Windsor Chairs

An Illustrated Celebration

Windsor Chairs

An Illustrated Celebration

Michael Harding-Hill

Antique Collectors' Club

©2003 Michael Harding-Hill
World copyright reserved

ISBN 1 85149 429 4

The right of Michael Harding-Hill to be identified as author of this work has been asserted by him in accordance with the Copyright, Designs and Patents Act 1988

All rights reserved. No part of this publication may be reproduced, stored in a retrieval system, or transmitted in any form or by any means electronic, mechanical, photocopying, recording or otherwise, without the prior permission of the publishers.

British Library Cataloguing-in-Publication Data
A catalogue record for this book is available from the British Library

Frontispiece. Late 18th century bow-back armchair. See page 48.
Title-page. The arms of Perceval and Compton from the 1756 chair on page 47.

Printed in Spain
by the Antique Collectors' Club Ltd., Woodbridge, Suffolk

ANTIQUE COLLECTORS' CLUB

The Antique Collectors' Club was formed in 1966 and quickly grew to a five figure membership spread throughout the world. It publishes the only independently run monthly antiques magazine, *Antique Collecting*, which caters for those collectors who are interested in widening their knowledge of antiques, both by greater awareness of quality and by discussion of the factors which influence the price that is likely to be asked. The Antique Collectors' Club pioneered the provision of information on prices for collectors and the magazine still leads in the provision of detailed articles on a variety of subjects.

It was in response to the enormous demand for information on 'what to pay' that the price guide series was introduced in 1968 with the first edition of *The Price Guide to Antique Furniture* (completely revised 1978 and 1989), a book which broke new ground by illustrating the more common types of antique furniture, the sort that collectors could buy in shops and at auctions rather than the rare museum pieces which had previously been used (and still to a large extent are used) to make up the limited amount of illustrations in books published by commercial publishers. Many other price guides have followed, all copiously illustrated, and greatly appreciated by collectors for the valuable information they contain, quite apart from prices. The Price Guide Series heralded the publication of many standard works of reference on art and antiques. *The Dictionary of British Art* (now in six volumes), *The Pictorial Dictionary of British 19th Century Furniture Design, Oak Furniture* and *Early English Clocks* were followed by many deeply researched reference works such as *The Directory of Gold and Silversmiths,* providing new information. Many of these books are now accepted as the standard work of reference on their subject.

The Antique Collectors' Club has widened its list to include books on gardens and architecture. All the Club's publications are available through bookshops world wide and a full catalogue of all these titles is available free of charge from the addresses below.

Club membership, open to all collectors, costs little. Members receive free of charge *Antique Collecting*, the Club's magazine (published ten times a year), which contains well-illustrated articles dealing with the practical aspects of collecting not normally dealt with by magazines. Prices, features of value, investment potential, fakes and forgeries are all given prominence in the magazine.

Among other facilities available to members are private buying and selling facilities and the opportunity to meet other collectors at their local antique collectors' clubs. There are over eighty in Britain and more than a dozen overseas. Members may also buy the Club's publications at special pre-publication prices.

As its motto implies, the Club is an organisation designed to help collectors get the most out of their hobby: it is informal and friendly and gives enormous enjoyment to all concerned.

For Collectors — By Collectors — About Collecting

ANTIQUE COLLECTORS' CLUB

www.antique-acc.com

Sandy Lane, Old Martlesham, Woodbridge, Suffolk, IP12 4SD, UK
Tel: (01394) 389950 Fax: (01394) 389999
Email: sales@antique-acc.com

or

Market Street Industrial Park, Wappingers' Falls, NY 12590, USA
Tel: 845 297 0003 Fax: 845 297 0068
Email: info@antiquecc.com

*... Yet this will go onward the same
Though Dynasties pass.*

Thomas Hardy, 'In Time of The Breaking Nations'

Contents

Acknowledgements	8
Foreword by John Andrews	9
Preface	10
Introduction	11
The Evolution of the Windsor Chair	15
The Eighteenth Century	16
Into the Nineteenth Century	86
The American Windsor	126
The Modern Tradition	140
Glossary	155
Select Bibliography	157
Index	158

ACKNOWLEDGEMENTS

I should like first of all to mention the late John Steel, whose suggestion it was, many years ago when I first became interested in Windsor chairs, that I should keep a good record of photographs, as the eighteenth century chairs in particular would become very rare. How right he turned out to be.

I should like to thank my cousin Geoffrey Yeo and Chris Baylis for their help and encouragement, also Primrose Elliott for her patience and Terry Pearson for the early work of collating and sorting out the pictures.

My thanks to Nicholas Grindley, John Boram, Noël Riley, Alan Mitchell, Paul Winsor, Stewart Linford, Bill Cotton, Roy Walker, John Andrews, Nancy Goyne Evans (for help with the introduction to the American section) and to the late Tom Crispin. All have helped, either by inspiration or encouragement.

Special thanks to the Wycombe Museum, the Victoria and Albert Museum, the National Maritime Museum, Greenwich, the Bodleian Library and the Henry Francis du Pont Winterthur Museum who all readily made available pictures from their libraries. Thanks too to Sir Edward Dashwood of West Wycombe Park (in the care of the National Trust) and to Stephen Tomlinson of the Bodleian Library for allowing me to photograph the chairs in situ, and to Mrs. Marigold MacRae of Eilean Donan Castle.

Finally thanks to all those who now own the chairs pictured in this book who so willingly gave their permission to my publishing pictures of their chairs.

All the photographs in the book, except where mentioned, were taken by Chris Challis.

To those I have missed out, please forgive me. This book has been a long time in the making and my memory is not what it was.

JOHN PERKS
1953–2002

Foreword

The Windsor chair is one of the most celebrated furniture creations of these islands, ranking alongside much eighteenth century furniture as a unique expression of design, construction and use of material. Its acceptance and utility led to its enthusiastic and early adoption in America, where original creativity led to a distinctly different set of forms but an equally celebrated industry.

Michael Harding-Hill has been established as a leading dealer and authority on the most desirable Windsor chairs for many years. To him have gone many collectors and enthusiasts in search of these 'Best Chairs' he describes in this book. No contemporary could have handled and assessed more Windsor chairs of high quality, observing and researching the remarkable range of features their makers lovingly incorporated as the form of chair developed over three centuries. It is indeed a wonderful piece of fortune for all Windsor chair fans that he has compiled a record of the remarkable chairs that have passed through his hands in the form of the sumptuous and mouthwatering illustrations made available to use in this luscious book.

This is not a conventional history of the Windsor chair, although the major facts are carefully recorded. It has a strong focus on the Thames Valley, since that is where the chair is said to have originated and, in the High Wycombe industry, has been so concentrated. Regional chairs, especially the best of the Worksop makers like John Gabbitass, fall within the range examined. The finest of American chairs find their place in a special chapter. What is unique about this book, however, is the extraordinary compilation of colour pictures of classic Thames Valley chairs in so many varieties. Michael Harding-Hill does not attempt to delve too far into technical, social and historical data. His is the view of a man who has developed an eye and a feeling for these chairs which everyone who loves them and seeks a record can understand.

It is hard to believe that the opportunity and experience needed to comprise such a masterly reference set can be undertaken by one man for many years to come. Anyone who does will need these illustrations. This book is a pictorial record far superior to any of those shown in previous works on the subject.

John Andrews

Preface

This small offering of a book deals with the beauty that craftsmen over the years have presented to history by their superb craftsmanship in chairmaking – the Windsor Chair. These chairs, whether simple or complicated in construction, plain or ornate in appearance, have always served their purpose, to be utilitarian, durable, comfortable and even handsome.

Many excellent academic works have been written on the subject and there is no attempt to improve on their expertise. The intention rather is to complement them by showing the finest designs in greater detail. The form and construction of the chairs speak for themselves. A major proportion of the chairs shown in this book, although in some cases two hundred years old, are still in use today. That is a wonder and worth recording. Is there another example of utilitarian furniture made in such numbers that still survives and is in everyday use? The illustrations that follow will more than prove the point.

Most of the chairs shown in this book have been in my possession, even if only for a short time. I have been able to look at them closely, to inspect the workmanship and to appreciate their beauty. There is no doubt in my mind that the Windsor could not be improved in any way.

This book is, therefore, a celebration of the Windsor chair.

INTRODUCTION

What is a Windsor chair?

The term Windsor chair is nowadays used to describe wooden chairs whose axis of construction is the seat, i.e. where the legs are jointed up into the underside of the seat board and the superstructure of the chair is jointed into the top of the seat board. The term Windsor chair thus includes hoop-back chairs of varying styles including the common wheel splat chair still found today in pubs and restaurants, various styles of 'kitchen' chairs as well as the more elegant eighteenth and nineteenth century hoop- and comb-back chairs predominantly featured in this book.

Why are they called Windsor chairs?
Nobody knows the exact answer, but there are many interesting theories. The most likely reason is that from early times stick chairs were being made in the Thames Valley area and Windsor was the distribution centre from where they were transported to London and most other places.

An unlikely theory is that George III, while out hunting in Windsor Great Park, sat in one whilst sheltering in a forester's cottage from a storm. In any case, these chairs were known as such some fifty years before George III came to the throne.

Evidence suggests that Windsor chairs were originally made as a relatively 'humble' form of seating. Their cheapness and lightness made them suitable for transportation far and wide away from the Thames Valley which established itself as the centre of the early Windsor chair making industry.

Written reference to early chairs tends to focus however on some of the more sophisticated styles which found their way into elegant surroundings.

One of the first recorded mentions of the Windsor chair as a specific type was by Lord Percival at Hall Barn, near Beaconsfield, Buckinghamshire, in 1724: '…the narrow winding walks and paths cut in it are innumerable and a woman in full health cannot walk them all, for which reason my wife was carry'd in a Windsor chair like those at Versailles, by which means she lost nothing worth seeing'.

Many eighteenth century English Windsor chairs are still providing practical and comfortable seating for modern day use in private homes and public places throughout the world. Notable

---

(Opposite.) A portrait by Edward Haytley (who exhibited at the Society of Artists of Great Britain 1760-1761) of Sir Roger and Lady Bradshaigh shows an early Windsor 'stick-back' in a comb-back form being used in the park of their Lancashire estate. The two chairs have been painted a drab green for garden use. Today, remains of original paint is a feature highly prized among collectors of eighteenth century Windsor chairs.

COURTESY OF WIGAN HERITAGE SERVICE

Introduction

Bills for 1756
Mr Munday for Chairs wallnuttree, 6 at 16 — 4:16:0
                Windsor 3 Doz at 8:6 — 15:06:0 } 20:02:00
Books &c.
   Mr Prince ——————————————————— 05:14:04
   Mr Fletcher ——————————————————— 11:11:00
   Bookbinders
= Carr. & moving Dr Rawlinson's Books
   Mr Parsons ——— 23:16:10   3:03:04
   Mr Sawney ——— 03:08:06
   pd by myself ———
Mr Wilkins Goldsmith. ———————————— 00:03:06
Smith's ————————————————————— 00:12:04
Bull Carpr & Schools ——— 07:01:07
Taylor Plumer & Glazr ——— 10:13:04
Blyfor Cabinet maker ——————————— 00:04:08
Medal of Alexr ye great ———————————— 00:10:06
Cole Glazier & Plumer 02:19:07
= Carr. of Dr R's Boxes by }
   Water pd by Mr Pottall } 00:19:03
5 Caps of Marble &c   01:16:00

West Wycombe Park, near High Wycombe, Buckinghamshire.

among many are the chairs in the Curator's Room of the Bodleian Library, Oxford (see also pages 28 and 29) which were made in 1756 and are still in use today.

Another example of eighteenth century Windsors in use today is at West Wycombe where the chairs are still under the same colonnade for which they were made. They were most probably made

---

(Opposite above.) The original chairs made for the Curator's Room in the Bodleian Library today.
CURATORS OF THE BODLEIAN LIBRARY

(Opposite below.) A page from the Bodleian Library daybook showing an entry, under Bills for 1756, for three dozen Windsor chairs. CURATORS OF THE BODLEIAN LIBRARY

Introduction

in the village of West Wycombe. Note the paint; these will have had many coats of paint over the last two hundred years or more and will have been taken out into the garden many times. What other piece of furniture made of wood could last so long and still look so elegant and be fit for use today?

The Evolution of the Windsor Chair

That we refer nowadays to the 'tradition' of Windsor chair making is an acknowledgement of the ongoing making of chairs of this style over time, and indeed the tradition is still alive today. The term tradition itself implies a history of an identifiable process. In the case of Windsor chair making the tradition as such becomes identifiable by the middle part of the eighteenth century when numerous craftsmen began to produce chairs of similar styles, using similar constructional methods. A rough overview can generalise:

a. The earliest stick-backs were comb-backs, mostly with simply turned legs, sometimes with cabriole legs.

b. The timbers used were fruitwood, walnut, ash and yew with seats almost always made from elm.

c. Predominantly armchairs were made.

d. Hoop-back armchairs were introduced whereby the outer back uprights and comb top were replaced by a hoop, similar in shape to the arm-bow.

e. Crinoline stretchers were favoured but in some cases an 'H' frame of delicate proportion with a finely turned middle stretcher was used.

f. Both stick-back and solid splat-back versions were made. The now common 'wheel' splat chair appeared only towards the end of the eighteenth century.

g. The beginning of the nineteenth century saw a shift, whereby certain styles of chairs were made predominantly in ash with some parts such as splats and sticks in fruitwood. Only 'better' or 'high quality' chairs were made in yew. The use of walnut declined. The seat remained elm. Side chairs began to be made in greater numbers.

h. Early chair makers probably made the whole chair themselves, but by the early part of the nineteenth century there is evidence to suggest that they 'bought in' certain parts from specialist 'part' makers, a tradition which became commonplace later in the century.

i. As the nineteenth century progressed chairs became bolder in feel, culminating in the middle of the century with the appearance of the square back chair, more commonly called 'kitchen' or 'farmhouse' chairs. They were robust in construction with curved cresting rails sitting on top of bold back uprights with slats, turned rails or sticks mixed with fretted splats in between. This was the time that the first standard 'slat-back' kitchen chair appeared. The use of beech became prevalent.

j. As the Industrial Revolution gathered pace so the chair maker's craft changed. It split into two almost separate traditions: one of the skilled high quality, low output maker and the other of 'assembly line', high volume makers.

k. The Windsor chair became increasingly a mass-production chair and in the early twentieth century was popular with civil and military institutions who bought mostly side chairs.

l. Although the mass-production makers have typically expanded their ranges into making all types of chairs, High Wycombe is still central to the Windsor chair making industry.

(Opposite.) Early stick chairs under the colonnaded south front of West Wycombe Park, in the 1930s (above) and still in use there today (below).

The Eighteenth Century – Stick-back Chairs

THE EIGHTEENTH CENTURY

STICK-BACK CHAIRS

The first written reference to a 'Windsor chair' was in 1724. Before this date they were probably referred to as 'stick furniture' and were made in a primitive form.

In 1727 John Brown, a chair maker and cabinet maker at the Three Chairs and Walnut Tree in St Paul's Churchyard, London, listed on his advertising card that he made 'All sorts of Windsor Garden chairs of all sizes painted green or in the wood'. The earliest type of the Windsor form of this period was probably the 'comb-back' and there are similar chairs of this early style still in use today (see page 14).

The earliest illustration of a 'Windsor' chair is a drawing c.1733 of an all stick comb-back type mounted on a platform enabling the weary and infirm to be wheeled around the gardens at Stowe in Buckinghamshire.

(Opposite.) The Rotunda at Stowe, c.1733, showing a comb-back Windsor on a wheeled platform.
COURTESY THE METROPOLITAN MUSEUM OF ART, NEW YORK

The Eighteenth Century

The following chair by John Pitt provides positive evidence that comb-back Windsor chairs with cabriole legs were being made by him in the middle of the eighteenth century.

Underside of the seat of the chair illustrated opposite showing a paper label and a metal plate. The poor condition label declares the maker to be John Pitt and continues *Wheelwright and Chairmaker …at SLO … DSO*, these letters being part of the words Slough and Windsor. John Pitt was buried on 13 January 1759. The metal plate states that *THIS CHAIR WENT WITH CAP. COOK AROUND THE WORLD*. Unfortunately it has not been possible to substantiate this claim. COURTESY CHRISTIE'S

(Opposite.) Mid-18th century comb-back arm chair. Attributed to Thames Valley region. Walnut and cherry wood, elm seat. COURTESY CHRISTIE'S

Another chair with recorded eighteenth century provenance is known as the Goldsmith chair. It was bequeathed by Oliver Goldsmith (1728-1774) to his friend William Hawes MD, founder of the Royal Humane Society. Nearly a century later the widow of Sir Benjamin Hawes (1797-1862), a descendant, presented it to the Victoria and Albert Museum, where it is today.

(Left.)
Windsor chair originally belonging to Oliver Goldsmith.
V&A PICTURE LIBRARY

(Opposite above.)
Stick-back chairs in the wardroom on board the *Gloucester,* c.1800.
©NATIONAL MARITIME MUSEUM, LONDON

(Opposite.)
Bible reading on board a British frigate by Augustus Earle (fl.1806-1838).
©NATIONAL MARITIME MUSEUM, LONDON

The Curators' chairs at the Bodleian Library in Oxford have already been mentioned in the introduction and the daybook entry of 1756 is an excellent provenance (see page 12).

Around this time contemporary paintings and sketches record that the Royal Navy had stick-back Windsor chairs as part of ships' furniture and there is a watercolour of Windsors in the wardroom on a warship. As inexpensive and light chairs they were ideal for this purpose and could be easily stored away when clearing the decks for action. There is supposed to have been a mention in a Royal Navy ship's log stating 'the Windsor chairs were taken up into the rigging when clearing for action'.

The Eighteenth Century

This is the Windsor chair at its most elaborate, a fine example of the Gothic so-called 'Chippendale' taste in country furniture. Note the fine tracery fretted splats, the well-formed cabriole legs and the pierced knee brackets.

A George II walnut Windsor armchair with baluster back, circa 1755. Rounded back, raised crest rails and a cipher 'HS' beneath an earl's coronet. Height of back 30in. (76cm), width 30½in. (77cm).

This is similar to a pair illustrated in *Masterpieces of English Furniture, The Gerstenfeld Collection* (Christie's Books, London 1998), sold at auction by Hurcombs, Piccadilly, London in May 1939 and at Christie's New York on 31 January 1981, lot 320 (the late Marjorie Wiggin Prescott). The Victoria & Albert Museum has another similar pair from the collection of Brigadier Clark, currently on loan to the National Trust at Mompesson House, Salisbury. See page 24 for illustrations of these. V&A PICTURE LIBRARY

There are many other recordings, pictures and illustrations of the Windsor chair from the early to late eighteenth century, mostly of what is known today as a 'comb back'.

Towards the late eighteenth century there is one of the first mentions of a 'bow-back'; surprisingly it is a wheel-back, which is generally thought to be nineteenth century. The Longridge bow-back, or hoop-back as it is known, has an inscription in ink underneath the seat board which reads: 'Mr Longridge, Gateshead Durham. 6 chairs by the Vulcan, Capt. R. Hawks, or by the first ship in that trade'. The purchaser of those six chairs (two of which are said to survive) was a Gateshead ironmaster, Thomas Longridge (1779-1803). Lloyds Shipping Register establishes delivery by the *Vulcan* between 1779 and 1783, but unfortunately does not name the maker. It does though prove that a bow-back chair with wheel fretted into the splat had been made around 1780.

Although there is no proof, we believe that the Gothic style chair illustrated on page 22 must have made an appearance around the 1760s. It is often referred to as the Strawberry Hill design after the house at Twickenham which was remodelled by Horace Walpole (1717-1797) and featured windows with a distinct Gothic shaping. The Gothic chair was almost always fashioned from yew wood. It is the most sophisticated and elegant of all Windsor chairs and today is the most sought after design.

The Eighteenth Century

Another similar pair, from the Collection of Brigadier Clark, currently on loan from the Victoria and Albert Museum to Mompesson House, Salisbury.
COURTESY THE NATIONAL TRUST – MOMPESSON HOUSE

One of a pair of chairs similar to that illustrated on page 23. Sold at auction by Hurcombs, Piccadilly, London in May 1939 and at Christie's New York on 31 January 1981, lot 320 (the late Marjorie Wiggin Prescott) and illustrated in *Masterpieces of English Furniture, The Gerstenfeld Collection* (Christie's Books, London 1998). COURTESY THE GERSTENFELD COLLECTION

In the mid-eighteenth century a new stylish chair design appeared, probably for use in the pleasure gardens that were becoming so fashionable. An inexpensive, light, strong and elegant form was needed to fulfil the requirement and the new design of Windsor chair with cabriole legs and bow back fitted the bill. They were soon adopted by other establishments such as tea rooms, coffee houses and the men's clubs that proliferated at the end of the eighteenth century.

The Windsor chair was now in use in the large estates, not only out of doors as the earlier chairs, but in the hall, the library and many other places where an economical, light, elegant chair was needed. Another major change about this time was that special chairs were made from yew and mahogany instead of mainly walnut, fruitwood and beech. The chair makers were sometimes even carving the legs and backs like the mahogany chairs of the day.

There are more examples of 18th provenance, all helping my belief that the Windsor chair was well established in everyday use well before 1800 and was already considered a fine and complete design. The Windsor chair had come of age.

I count it a privilege to have handled nearly all of these chairs and to have had the opportunity of examining their craftsmanship in close detail.

(Opposite.) The classic Thames Valley cabriole-legged bow-back Windsor elbow chair, late 18th century. However, this very rare chair has extra enhancements such as the carved knee and foot (see close-ups on page 64), features more readily associated with more formal chairs.

The Eighteenth Century

The Eighteenth Century – Stick-back Chairs

Mid-18th century simple walnut stick-back side chair or back stool, stool base.
CURATORS OF THE BODLEIAN LIBRARY

(Opposite.) Another view. The disc underneath is a later addition to strengthen the worn seat. Note that the shape of the leg is similar to the following example. CURATORS OF THE BODLEIAN LIBRARY

The Eighteenth Century – Stick-back Chairs

The Eighteenth Century – Stick-back Chairs

Mid-18th century stick-back elbow chair, circa 1766. Mainly ash, elm seat

This is almost certainly one of the set made for the Bodleian about which a letter in *Jackson's Oxford Journal* of 29 November 1766 noted 'The Bodleian Library has most confessedly been very much improved by the introduction of Windsor Chairs so admirably calculated for ornament and repose' (see pages 12 and 13).

CURATORS OF THE BODLEIAN LIBRARY

Another view of the chair opposite.
CURATORS OF THE BODLEIAN LIBRARY

Detail showing the underarm support.
CURATORS OF THE BODLEIAN LIBRARY

The Eighteenth Century – Stick-back Chairs

Mid-18th century comb-back (all sticks) elbow chair. Mahogany. Height 41in. (104cm). Width 23in. (58cm)
This chair is unusual as it is all mahogany. It was probably meant to be used indoors, say in a library or as a hall chair, and not outside.

Mid-18th century comb-back (all sticks) elbow chair. Attributed to Thames Valley region, circa 1760. Yew wood, elm seat. Height 38in. (97cm). Width 19in. (48cm)
This comb-back Windsor elbow chair, with its turned legs joined by an 'H' stretcher and its simple crest rail, is a classic form of the late 18th century. This style of chair has been recorded in beech and was probably painted for garden use.

(Opposite.)
Late 18th century comb-back (all sticks) elbow chair. Attributed to Thames Valley region
Fruitwood, elm seat. Height 37in. (94cm). Width 19in. (48cm)
This late 18th century comb-back chair has cabriole front legs which are joined by an 'H' stretcher. The crest rail is more pronounced in shape and the swept back underarm supports allow more room for the larger person. Though a small chair, it is very handsome.

The Eighteenth Century – Stick-back Chairs

The Eighteenth Century – Stick-back Chairs

18th century matched set of six comb-back elbow chairs. Attributed to Thames Valley region, circa 1780. Fruitwood, elm seats. Height 38in. (97cm). Width 19in. (48cm)

The Eighteenth Century – Stick-back Chairs

Mid-18th century original set of six double bow chairs. Attributed to Thames Valley region, circa 1780. Yew wood, fruitwood, elm seats. Height 38in. (97cm). Width 20in. (51cm)
This original set of six double bow Windsor chairs is extremely rare.

The Eighteenth Century – Stick-back Chairs

18th century double bow elbow chair. Attributed to Thames Valley region, circa 1770. Yew wood, fruitwood, elm seat. Height 36in. (91cm). Width 20in. (51cm)
Simple form of double bow stick-back similar to those on the previous page but with a crinoline stretcher.

(Opposite.) 18th century double bow elbow chair. Attributed to Thames Valley region, circa 1770. Walnut, elm seat. Height 38in. (97cm). Width 20in. (51cm)
This beautiful walnut double bow Windsor chair has four cabriole legs which are joined by a turned 'H' stretcher. The arm bow is made in three pieces, with a shaped raised back section. It has outward sweeping ends finishing in a shaped undercut. A chair such as this shows off to the best advantage the chair maker's art – of the (stick-back) form there is no better design. It looks good from any angle and as such was surely an important household chair.

18th century double bow elbow chair, Attributed to Thames Valley region, circa 1770. Yew wood, fruitwood, elm seat. Height 36in. (91cm). Width 20in. (51cm). Single similar to the set on page 33.

The Eighteenth Century – Stick-back Chairs

The Eighteenth Century – Solid Splat Chairs

SOLID SPLAT CHAIRS

Late 18th century comb-back elbow chair. Attributed to Thames Valley region. Fruitwood, elm seat. Height 43in. (109cm). Width 21in. (53cm)
Shaped crest rail, vase-shaped splat and well-drawn turned legs.

(Opposite.) Late 18th century comb-back elbow chair. Attributed to Thames Valley region. Fruitwood, ash, elm seat. Height 42in. (107cm). Width 20in. (51cm)
It has very simple cabriole legs and a pleasant angular vase-shaped splat.

The Eighteenth Century – Solid Splat Chairs

The Eighteenth Century – Solid Splat Chairs

The Eighteenth Century – Solid Splat Chairs

Pair of mid-18th century comb-back side chairs. Attributed to Thames Valley region. Fruitwood, ash, elm seat. Height 37in. (94cm). Width 18in. (46cm)
Very simple crest rail back supports, bold cabriole legs, wedge with rods for extra support to back. Previously unrecorded. A favourite of mine.

(Opposite.) 18th century comb-back elbow chair. Attributed to Thames Valley region, circa 1770. Fruitwood, ash, elm seat. Height 38in. (97cm). Width 19in. (48cm)
Very pronounced cabriole leg, wedge with rods for extra support to back of chair. A very individual chair.

The Eighteenth Century – Solid Splat Chairs

Late 18th century comb-back elbow chair. Attributed to Thames Valley region. Fruitwood, ash, elm seat. Height 43in. (109cm). Width 21in. (53cm)
Shaped crest rail, turned legs, vase-shaped splat, 'H' stretcher.

Almost identical to the provenanced John Pitt chair illustrated on page 19.

(Opposite.)
Late 18th century comb-back elbow chair. Attributed to Thames Valley region. Fruitwood, ash, elm seat. Height 39in. (99cm). Width 25in. (64cm)
An impressive example of an 18th century English comb-back Windsor chair with a vase splat. It has four cabriole legs each with carved hoof feet and showing stylised 'fetlocks'. An 'H' stretcher joins the legs. Incurved flat shaped underarm supports. Its central splat is of Queen Anne style and, with its two sticks and an outer slat either side, together forms the comb-back. The superb yoke-shaped crest rail adds to the rarity of this very fine chair.

The Eighteenth Century – Solid Splat Chairs

Mid-18th century pair of comb-back side chairs. Attributed to Thames Valley region. Fruitwood, elm seat. Height 37in. (94cm). Width 17in. (43cm)
Elaborately shaped crest rail, bold cabriole legs, turned leg stretchers, vase-shaped splat. These side chairs were presumably made to be supplied in sets – see opposite for the matching carvers.

The Eighteenth Century – Solid Splat Chairs

Mid-18th century pair of comb-back elbow chairs. Attributed to Thames Valley region. Fruitwood, walnut, ash, elm seat. Height 43in. (109cm). Width 21in. (53cm)
Elaborately shaped crest rail, bold cabriole legs, turned leg stretchers, vase-shaped splat. See opposite for side chairs of this style of comb-back and see also page 44 for a set of eight, collected and matched by the author.

The Eighteenth Century – Solid Splat Chairs

The Eighteenth Century – Solid Splat Chairs

(Opposite.)
18th century matched set of ten comb-back chairs, eight side chairs, two elbow chairs. Attributed to Thames Valley region, circa 1770. Fruitwood, elm seats.

18th century comb-back elbow chair. Attributed to Thames Valley region, circa 1770. Fruitwood, walnut, ash, elm seat. Height 43in. (109cm). Width 21in. (53cm)
The underarm supports are shaped, the legs are nicely turned, and the vase splat is very finely shaped. Probably used as carvers and supplied in sets with the chair on the left as well as single elbow chairs.

18th century comb-back side chair. Attributed to Thames Valley region, circa 1770. Fruitwood, elm seat. Height 37in. (94cm). Width 17in. (43cm)
Shaped crest rail, simple turned legs, and vase-shaped splat. These side chairs were probably made to be supplied in sets – see above for the elbow chairs, which would have been used as the carvers.

The Eighteenth Century – Solid Splat Chairs

Late 18th century bow-back armchair.
An unusually large splat with some simple fretting, the top shaped area of which has been painted with an armorial. A crinoline stretcher joins its turned legs. Swept back underarm supports. This Windsor chair was again possibly used as a hall chair, but could also have been used for sitting out in the garden – under a veranda (see page 14) or in a gazebo or arbour – on one of the great English estates.

Late 18th century comb-back elbow chair. Attributed to Thames Valley region. Fruitwood, beech, elm seat.
Swept back underarm supports, turned legs united by a turned stretcher. Vase splat only above the arm bow, which has an armorial crest painted on to the splat. Possibly used as a hall or garden chair.   COURTESY LADY D'ALBIAC

The Eighteenth Century – Solid Splat Chairs

The armorial on the left-hand chair opposite.

Armchair dated 1756 and bearing the arms of Perceval and Compton, decorated for the marriage of Egmont and Compton. See title-page for close-up of the arms.
V&A PICTURE LIBRARY

The crest of the D'Albiac family on the right-hand chair opposite.

47

The Eighteenth Century – Solid Splat Chairs

Late 18th century bow-back armchair chair. Attributed to Thames Valley region. Yew wood, ash, elm seat. Height 40in. (102cm). Width 19in. (48cm)
Bold cabriole legs joined by a crinoline stretcher, unusual vase splat.

(Opposite.)
18th century comb-back elbow chair. Attributed to Thames Valley region, circa 1770. Walnut, fruitwood, elm seat. Height 41in. (104cm). Width 20in. (51cm)
Simple crest rail, plain cabriole legs joined by a turned 'H' stretcher, swept back underarm supports. It has a very simple shaped splat and an unusual all slat (rather than sticks) construction. Previously unrecorded.

Late 18th century comb-back elbow chair. Attributed to the West Country. Yew wood, ash, elm seat. Height 40in. (102cm). Width 22in. (56cm)
Unusual cabriole legs, shaped underarm supports, vase splat.

The Eighteenth Century – Solid Splat Chairs

The Eighteenth Century – Solid Splat Chairs

(Above.)
Late 18th century comb-back elbow chair. Attributed to Thames Valley region. Ash, elm seat. Height 41in. (104cm). Width 23in. (58cm)
Curved crest rail, the turned legs finish in a pad foot, the underarm supports are very elaborate. It has a very well defined seat. Most unusual is the lack of stretchers. There are many features similar to the chair on the right.

(Opposite.)
Late 18th century comb-back elbow chair. Attributed to Thames Valley region. Fruitwood, walnut, ash, elm seat. Height 43in. (109cm). Width 21in. (53cm)
Beautiful arm bow made in three pieces with shaped raised back section and outward sweeping ends finishing in a shaped undercut. The underarm supports and legs have unusually shaped turning.

(Below.)
Late 18th century bow-back elbow chair. Attributed to Thames Valley region. Ash, elm seat. Height 43in. (109cm). Width 21in. (53cm)
This chair is most unusual. Its one piece splat is very fine, the turned legs finish in pad feet which face forward, the underarm supports are very elaborate. The pleasant bow shape itself with the ten sticks is uncommon and it has a very well defined seat. All these unusual features combine to make this an extraordinary but beautiful chair.

FRETTED CHAIRS

The Eighteenth Century – Fretted Chairs

Detail of fixings on the left-hand chair.

Late 18th century double bow elbow chair. Attributed to Thames Valley region. Yew wood, fruitwood, elm seat. Height 38in. (97cm). Width 19in. (48cm)

Late 18th century style turned legs, joined by a crinoline stretcher. It is of a double bow construction and has swept back underarm supports. The central splat is fairly simple but elegant. This particular chair has fixings that possibly indicate it had a headrest at one time (see detail).

(Opposite.) Mid-18th century armchair. Mahogany. Height 40in. (102cm). Width 22in. (56cm)

This superb chair at first glance doesn't appear to be a Windsor, but it is as both the legs and superstructure are jointed into the seat board. See 'What is a Windsor Chair?' (page 11).

Late 18th century double bow elbow chair. Attributed to Thames Valley and Chilterns region. Yew wood, fruitwood, elm seat. Height 48in. (122cm). Width 20in. (51cm)

Late 18th century style turned legs, joined by a crinoline stretcher. Its double bow construction is much sturdier than the previous chair and the very high back and splendid fretted central splat give this chair an important look. There were several designs within the central splat of this style of chair, this one being The Prince of Wales' feathers.

The Eighteenth Century – Fretted Chairs

Late 18th century double bow elbow chair. Attributed to Thames Valley region. Yew wood, fruitwood, elm seat. Height 40in. (102cm). Width 20in. (51cm)
Double bow with fretted vase shaped central splat. This a more sophisticated chair than the previous example. The chair maker's skill in adding more sticks to the back of the chair and turning the back legs creates a more stylish chair. This is a good looking chair and many of this type would have been used in coffee houses, good taverns and even in large houses as hall chairs or library chairs.

Late 18th century double bow elbow chair. Attributed to Thames Valley region. Yew wood, fruitwood, elm seat. Height 38in. (97cm). Width 19in. (48cm)
In most ways similar to the left-hand chair on page 53, but with cabriole legs.

(Opposite.)
Late 18th century double bow elbow chair. Attributed to the Thames Valley region. Yew wood, fruitwood, elm seat. Height 41in. (104cm). Width 20in. (51cm)
A classic Thames Valley double bow Windsor chair. The splat relates to designs published by Thomas Chippendale in *The Gentleman and Cabinet-Maker's Director* in 1754. The superb cabriole legs are joined to the simple rear legs by a crinoline stretcher. These highly stylised chairs are believed to be of the type that were used in the pleasure gardens, coffee houses and tea rooms in and around London and the provincial fashionable cities during the late 18th century. These and the others of this style are probably the most beautiful of all the Windsor chair family.

The Eighteenth Century – Fretted Chairs

55

The Eighteenth Century – Fretted Chairs

Late 18th century double bow elbow chairs. Thames Valley region. Yew wood, fruitwood, elm seat. Height 41in. (104cm). Width 20in. (51cm)
A pair of classic Thames Valley double bow Windsor chairs. These splat designs, again a variant of a Chippendale style, are the only difference from the previous chair.

(Opposite.)
Late 18th century double bow elbow chairs. Thames Valley region. Yew wood, fruitwood, elm seat. Height 41in. (104cm). Width 20in. (51cm)
A matched set of six elbow chairs of the same design and style.

The Eighteenth Century – Fretted Chairs

57

The Eighteenth Century – Fretted Chairs

Late 18th century double bow elbow chairs. Thames Valley region. Yew wood, fruitwood, elm seat. Height 41in. (104cm). Width 20in. (51cm)
Both are types of the classic Thames Valley double bow elbow chair with Chippendale style splat.

(Opposite.)
Late 18th century double bow elbow chair. Thames Valley region. Yew wood, fruitwood, elm seat. Height 41in. (104cm). Width 20in. (51cm)
This has an armorial painted on the central splat associating it with one of the 18th century great English estates.

Detail of the armorial.

The Eighteenth Century – Fretted Chairs

The Eighteenth Century – Fretted Chairs

Late 18th century double bow elbow chairs. Thames Valley region. Yew wood, fruitwood, elm seat. Height 41in. (104cm). Width 23in. (58cm)
An original pair of large classic Thames Valley double bow Windsor chairs, differing from the one on page 55 only in the splat designs, which are again Chippendale in style. This pair of chairs could well have been made as a special order. As far as the author knows, no other pair of chairs this size and in this style have been recorded. They truly are a wonderful pair of chairs and a credit to the chair maker responsible for their manufacture.

The Eighteenth Century – Fretted Chairs

Late 18th century double bow elbow chair. Thames Valley region. Yew wood, fruitwood, elm seat. Height 41in. (104cm). Width 20in. (51cm)
Single chair similar to that on page 55.

Late 18th century double bow elbow chair. Thames Valley region. Yew wood, fruitwood, elm seat. Height 38in. (97cm). Width 19in. (48cm)
Single chair similar to those on page 56, but much smaller. It has an 'H' stretcher and the fretted splat is more elaborate.

The Eighteenth Century – Fretted Chairs

Late 18th century double bow elbow chair. Thames Valley region. Yew wood, fruitwood, elm seat. Height 41in. (104cm). Width 20in. (51cm)
Single chair similar to that on page 55.

The Eighteenth Century – Fretted Chairs

Late 18th century double bow elbow chair. Thames Valley region. Yew wood, fruitwood, elm seat. Height 41in. (104cm). Width 20in. (51cm)
Single chair similar to those on page 56.

The Eighteenth Century – Fretted Chairs

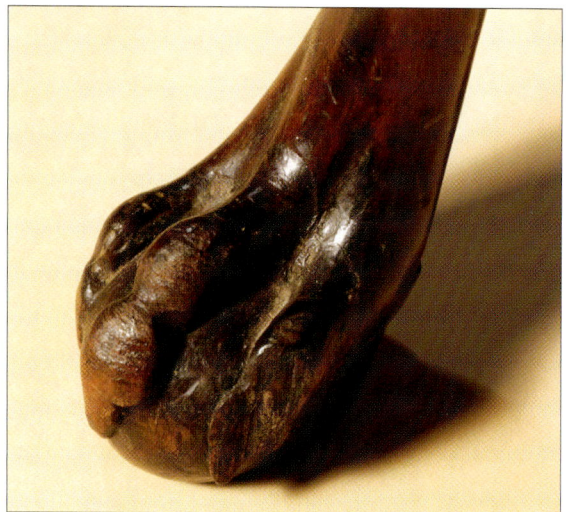

Carved foot.

Carved knee.

Carved cabriole leg.

(Opposite.)
Late 18th century double bow elbow chair. Thames Valley region. Yew wood, fruitwood, elm seat. Height 41in. (104cm). Width 20in. (51cm)
The classic Thames Valley cabriole-legged bow-back Windsor elbow chair. However, this very rare chair has extra enhancements such as the carved knee and foot (see details above), which is most unusual on a Windsor chair. These refinements are normally found on the upholstered chairs of the period. This chair is most rare and could have been made for a special purpose. Though chairs with carving such as this have been recorded, they have been in walnut or mahogany. This style of chair with such sophisticated carving in yew wood to date is unrecorded.

The Eighteenth Century – Fretted Chairs

65

Mid-18th century elbow chair. Attributed to Thames Valley region. Yew wood, mahogany seat. Height 42½in. (106cm). Width 22in. (56cm)
A bellflower and flowerhead carved hoop back and pierced interlaced vase-shaped splat carved with wheat ears, rosettes and floral swags, with inswept front arm supports, a mahogany shaped seat with conforming carved front edge, on anthemion carved cabriole legs with pad feet and joined by a crinoline stretcher.

COURTESY CHRISTIE'S

The Eighteenth Century – Fretted Chairs

Late 18th century comb-back elbow chair. Attributed to the Thames Valley region. Fruitwood, elm seat. Height 41in. (104cm). Width 22in. (56cm)
Front cabriole legs joined by an exceptionally well-turned 'H' stretcher, highly decorated crest rail and an unusual central fretted splat. The underarm supports are well swept back, most probably to allow the sitter more thigh room. Note also that it has a ribbon slat, as do most comb-backs.

The Eighteenth Century – Fretted Chairs

Late 18th century comb-back elbow chair. Attributed to the Thames Valley region. Fruitwood, elm seat. Height 42in. (107cm). Width 22in. (56cm)

Another style of comb-back chair. As with most comb-back Windsors, the front cabriole legs are joined by an 'H' stretcher. It has a simpler crest rail and the splat design, which is very similar to the one on page 63, appears to continue the Chippendale style. It has a ribbon slat, as most comb-backs, the underarm supports are shaped and the back legs have been turned. A very stylish chair.

The Eighteenth Century – Fretted Chairs

Mid-18th century comb-back elbow chair. Fruitwood, elm seat. Height 44in. (112cm). Width 21in. (54cm)
This chair, although circa 1780, has many features found on the earlier Windsors. The simple cabriole front legs are less sophisticated and the turned 'H' stretchers and back legs appear more primitive. The bow, which is constructed from three sections, with its raised back section is a form generally associated with the West Country and the early comb-back chairs. Also note the ribbon slat at either side of the sticks which is common to most comb-backs and which presumably gave a little extra strength, also the shaped underarm supports. Unusually, the two sticks under the arm have been turned. The splat is similar in many ways to that on page 67.

The Eighteenth Century – Fretted Chairs

Mid-18th century comb-back elbow chair. Attributed to the Thames Valley region. Fruitwood, elm seat. Height 44in. (112cm). Width 21in. (54cm)
This chair is very similar to the previous example, except for the splat which in this case has a bell in the fretted design, and the underarm support.

The Eighteenth Century – Fretted Chairs

Mid-18th century comb-back elbow chair. Attributed to the Thames Valley region. Fruitwood, elm seat. Height 44in. (112cm). Width 21in. (53cm)
This chair is very similar to the previous two. It too has a fretted bell though no cross under. The main difference with this chair is an early feature of carved feet, as in the lower chair on page 40.

(Above left.)
Fretted splat.

(Left.)
Cabriole leg showing carved foot.

The Eighteenth Century – Fretted Chairs

The Eighteenth Century – Fretted Chairs

An exceptionally rare original set of six late 18th century comb-back Windsor chairs.

Late 18th century comb-back elbow chair. Attributed to the Thames Valley region. Fruitwood, elm seat. Height 44in. (112cm). Width 21in. (53cm)
A single example from the set above.

The Eighteenth Century – Fretted Chairs

Late 18th century comb-back elbow chair. Attributed to the Thames Valley region. Fruitwood, elm seat. Height 44in. (112cm). Width 21in. (53cm)
An impressive example of an 18th century English comb-back Windsor chair with a Chippendale-style fretted splat. It has four cabriole legs, joined by an 'H' stretcher, and incurved flat-shaped underarm supports. Its central splat is flanked by four sticks and the comb back is supported by an outer slat on either side.

The Eighteenth Century – Fretted Chairs

Late 18th century double bow elbow chair. Attributed to the Thames Valley region. Yew, fruitwood and elm. Height 44in. (112cm). Width 21in. (53cm)
Another impressive example of an 18th century English double bow Windsor chair with a Chippendale-style fretted splat. It has four cabriole legs joined by a crinoline stretcher, and swept back underarm supports. Its central splat has three sticks and an outer slat either side which is enclosed by the top bow.

The Eighteenth Century – Fretted Chairs

The Eighteenth Century – Fretted Chairs

(Left.)
Late 18th century double bow elbow chair. Thames Valley region.
Similar to the chair on page 62.
COURTESY MR. AND MRS. R. PARROTT COLLECTION

(Below.)
Late 18th century comb-back chair with cabriole legs and a very simple central splat. Thames Valley region.
COURTESY MR. AND MRS. R. PARROTT COLLECTION

(Opposite.)
Mid-18th century comb-back elbow chair, circa 1740. Fruitwood, elm seat. Height 39in. (99cm). Width 32in. (81cm)
An important and rare mahogany armchair on four cabriole legs, with outswept arms and shaped cresting rail. As the legs are jointed to the underside of the seat and the back and arms are joined to the seat it can be classed as a Windsor chair. The quality of construction of this chair, with its massive seat and scroll detail, and its beautifully drawn cabriole legs, suggests a major cabinetmaker of the period.
COURTESY J. WEBER COLLECTION
PHOTOGRAPH STEPHEN JARRETT

The Eighteenth Century – Fretted Chairs

Trade card of William Webb (fl.1792-1808) who worked in Newington, Surrey. Note the similarity of the chair in the top right corner to the 'X' frame chair illustrated opposite.

'X' frame chair with Windsor elements, such as the arm bow, splat, sticks and underarm supports. Circa 1800.

This very rare chair was probably a veranda or garden chair. The paint is original and is in the late 18th/early 19th century style. I have never seen a chair of this style before and, as far as I know, it has not been previously recorded.

Although 'X' frame chairs have existed from the 16th century, the inspiration for the unusual leg arrangement is clearly from a Regency 'X' framed stool.

COURTESY ROBERT HIRSCHHORN, PHOTOGRAPH ROY FARTHING

The Eighteenth Century – Fretted Chairs

79

Gothic Chairs

The Gothic Windsor chair is generally considered to be among the best Windsor furniture. It is almost always made of yew wood.

This chair was always a 'Best Chair' and would have been used in taverns, university colleges and other such places where it would have been held in high regard as an example of fine 18th century furniture. Highly prized today, and the most sought-after style of Windsor chair, it is quintessentially English and looks superb in most settings.

(Opposite.)
This is the Windsor chair at its most elaborate, a fine example of the so-called 'Chippendale' taste in country furniture. Note the fine tracery fretted splats, the well-formed cabriole legs and the pierced knee brackets.

The Eighteenth Century – Gothic Chairs

Mid-18th century Gothic Windsor elbow chair. Attributed to Thames Valley region, circa 1760. Yew wood, fruitwood, elm seat. Height 41in. (104cm). Width 22in. (56cm)

Double bow construction. The tracery design owes much to the 18th century Gothic Revival. The underarm supports and the front and turned legs are very finely shaped, the underarm supports being particularly interesting. No recorded period Gothic Windsor chair has yet been found in any wood other than the prized yew wood (the seat, though, is still made from elm). This extremely rare chair is from the mid- to late 18th century.

The Eighteenth Century – Gothic Chairs

18th century Gothic elbow chair. Attributed to Thames Valley region, circa 1770. Yew wood, fruitwood, elm seat. Height 42in. (107). Width 21in. (53cm)
This style of Windsor has been considered for some time to be the pinnacle of Windsor chair design; it is more sought after than any other Windsor chair, and is rarer than any of the other styles.

This chair is of the more usual Gothic chair construction, having the top bow made in two parts which creates the Gothic arch from which it gets its name.

The Eighteenth Century – Gothic Chairs

Mid-18th century triple arch Gothic Windsor settee and matching elbow chairs. Attributed to Thames Valley region, circa 1760. Yew wood, elm seat. Height 40in. (102cm). Width 64in. (163cm)
The settee is a very rare and exciting example of Windsor furniture of the mid-18th century.
COURTESY MICHAEL GOLDING
(HUNTINGTON ANTIQUES)

18th century Gothic elbow chair. Attributed to Thames Valley region, circa 1770. Yew wood, fruitwood, elm seat. Height 42in. (107cm). Width 22in. (56cm)
Similar to the chair on page 83, but with a less pointed arch back and a wider and more prominent seat. Also, the turnings on the back legs are lower down. A grander chair, perhaps.

(Opposite.)
18th century Gothic elbow chair. Attributed to Thames Valley region, circa 1770. Yew wood, fruitwood, elm seat. Height 40in. (102cm). Width 20in. (51cm)
Double bow construction, similar to the chair on page 82. This chair, though, has cabriole front legs, which are joined by a crinoline stretcher, and also swept back underarm supports. It is smaller than usual, but nevertheless a very attractive looking chair.

Eilean Donan Castle, near Dornie, Ross-shire (see page 88).

INTO THE NINETEENTH CENTURY

Until the end of the eighteenth century the Windsor chair making tradition was typified by numerous individual makers spread throughout the Thames Valley, making all chair parts and assembling the whole in their own workshops.

At the turn of the nineteenth century, as High Wycombe and the surrounding villages confirmed their position as the centre for the southern chair making industry, the practice of piecework making of chair components became common place; the larger chair workshops would buy in many of the chair parts from individual 'bodgers' and 'turners' in readiness for assembly and framing into the finished article. It is said that by 1877 over four thousand five hundred chairs a day were produced in High Wycombe – the equivalent of over one million chairs a year – and this from one area alone.

Other areas outside the Thames Valley also emerged as centres of the chair making industry, notably the Worksop and Rockley areas of Nottinghamshire and Sleaford and Grantham in Lincolnshire. Although the basic methods of construction remained the same for the chairs made in these areas, there were significant differences.

It is possible to identify some chairs by certain features in their design as being from a specific area or by a specific maker. Indeed, some of the chair makers stamped their names on their chairs. One of the first Worksop chair makers, John Gabbitass (fl.1822-39), branded the underside of the seat board with his name (see below). Gabbitass made what is arguably the best nineteenth century low-back (see page 94). After his death his widow Elizabeth Gabbitass carried on the business (1839-44), the only recorded woman to run a chair workshop. The chairs during her time were stamped on the edge of the seat board 'E. Gabbitass, Worksop'.

The stamp John Gabbitass (fl.1822-39) branded on the underside of the seat board of his chairs.

The Nineteenth Century

Wilson Windsor chairs in the Banqueting Hall, Eilean Donan Castle.

Other Worksop families, such as J. Godfrey and J. Allsop, also made high quality yew wood Windsors, often referred to as 'Best Chairs'.

Another maker who stamped his chairs was George Wilson (fl.1841-91) of Grantham. Ten of his elbow chairs now grace the Banqueting Hall of the romantic Eilean Donan Castle in Ross-shire, family furniture brought to the castle when it was restored from 1912-1932.

The history of many of the makers is intriguing and I can heartily recommend Dr. Bernard Cotton's extensive work, *The English Regional Chair*, published by the Antique Collectors' Club, for those who wish to take a more academic approach to this subject.

From the illustrations that follow it is evident that the Northern chair makers developed a more robust construction than those in the South. Northern chairs featured bold turnings under the arms instead of the finer curved underarm supports normally found in their southern tradition counterparts. In armchairs the central fretted splat was typically made in two pieces, with both parts being jointed into a mortise hole bored through the arm bow, in contrast to the southern tradition of jointing a one-piece splat into the front of the arm bow, leaving the full length face visible. Those manufacturers nearer London were perhaps more easily able to observe the design of the fashionable cabinet makers and consequently developed a lighter style with some of the splats celebrating events of the day and emulating current fashion.

The stamp of George Wilson, Grantham (fl.1841-91).

The Nineteenth Century

The Thames Valley, Nottinghamshire and Lincolnshire remained the consistent centres of Windsor chair making throughout the first half of the nineteenth century. There is evidence of a less well-established tradition in the West Country and isolated and specific traditions were established in other areas. For instance, Mendlesham in Suffolk was a centre of production of a most individual style of chair (see page 90).

The rise of mass-production methods towards the end of the nineteenth century with the introduction of machines and improved distribution created the conditions for the Windsor chair to become a truly national utilitarian piece of furniture. Many municipal and government authorities were not slow to appreciate their utility and purchased them for public use. Windsor chairs found themselves used in offices, schools and many public institutions. The military were buyers in quantity and, as if to illustrate the infinite adaptability of the basic design, a chair was produced with only one arm to accommodate officers' dress swords.

The military sent the chairs, possibly in kit form, all over the world. The Navy also continued to supply Windsor chairs to its ship and shore bases.

A chair produced for the military, with only one arm to accommodate officers' dress swords.

The Nineteenth Century

Tradition has it that Mendlesham chair making was started by a certain Dan Day, a local wheelwright, at the end of the eighteenth century. His son, Richard, was supposed to have been apprenticed to Sheraton and to have then returned to Suffolk and carried on his father's chair making business. As Sheraton probably never had a furniture making workshop of his own but was, according to his trade card, a teacher of 'Perspective, Architecture and Ornaments', a maker of 'Designs for Cabinet-makers' and a seller of 'all kinds of Drawing Books, etc.', this is most unlikely. However, it is possible that Dan Day's son took drawing lessons from Sheraton, a theory reinforced by the elegant – one could say Sheratonesque – lines of the Mendlesham chair back.

It is perhaps more likely that the young Day was apprenticed to one of the many London chair makers of the period and later returned to Suffolk to help his father.

Quite a large cluster of Days is revealed in the Mendlesham parish records, beginning with Robert Day, who married Susan Ottowell in 1756 and whose children, Mary, Susan and Robert, were baptised in the church there in 1757, 1760 and 1761 respectively. Another branch of the family was headed by Richard (1749-1812) who married Mary Potter (d.1816) and produced Mary, Richard (1785-1838), Robert and another Mary (perhaps the first had died young). It seems most likely that this latter Richard, of apprenticeship age in the late eighteenth and the first few years of the nineteenth century, would have ben the one taught by Sheraton – or a London chairmaker of his period – rather than his father.

However, no mention of a Daniel Day seems to occur and our Richard Day's father was also called Richard. Is it possible that he was really 'Dick' and not the 'Dan' Day of local tradition, and that the shortened form of his name changed misleadingly into Dan in the course of decades of the spoken rather than the written word? Indeed, more than one source of information refers to these chairs as 'Dick' Day chairs instead of the more usual Dan Day. By no means everyone seems to be agreed on whether Dan or Dick and Richard Day were in fact father and son or brothers, and at least one writer mentions the brothers 'John and Dan Day'.

The first Mendlesham chairs were probably made in the last decade of the eighteenth century, although it is hard to be precise when dating traditional forms of furniture, and they may have been later. Certainly most extant examples are datable to the first thirty years of the nineteenth century. On the tithe map of 1839 the Day's house and workshop mentioned by a local antique dealer in 1943 as 'still standing a few years ago' was occupied not by the Days, but by a certain Edmund Jacob, and all available evidence points to the death of Richard Day junior in 1838 as the end of the Day family's involvement with chair making.

Between about 1830 and 1850 other makers were almost certainly producing chairs of the Mendlesham type. Among them the names Scott of Diss, Harold of Seall, and Leggat have been put forward. Suffolk trade directories between the 1840s and '70s give no further clues and the last Mendlesham chairs were probably produced in the 1850s.

Taken from a paper by Noël Riley, 'The Mysterious Mendlesham chair'

(Above.)
One of a set of six single fruitwood and elm Mendlesham chairs. PRIVATE COLLECTION

(Opposite.)
Two Mendlesham armchairs Both are of basic form, with turned legs.

The Nineteenth Century

Tablet form Windsor armchairs
These are identical to the chairs made for the reading rooms of the Bodleian Library, Oxford. Two of the makers known to have made and supplied chairs to the Library are S. Hazell of Oxford and Glenister's Chair Manufacture in High Wycombe.

An armchair of this design stamped Webb and Bunce (1804-32) has also been recorded.

Some makers, notably Stephen Hazell (1846-92), produced singular types of Windsor chairs for specific places such as the reading rooms of the Bodleian Library and some of the colleges in Oxford. After 1900 Glenister's of High Wycombe took on the supply to the Bodleian.

There were other special Windsor chairs and several sizes, from small child's size through adolescence to giant size. Although content to mass-produce to a price, chair makers still made special or 'Best Chairs' to a much higher specification than the run-of-the-mill chairs. These catered for the growing more affluent sector of society and the most favoured wood for these chairs was yew. Some chairs, I suspect, were made to prove or satisfy the chair makers' desire to show they were still capable of making good chairs and doubtless some local or area rivalries existed.

Typical examples of these higher quality or, to use the contemporary term, 'Best', chairs are shown.

Again I can claim that virtually all the chairs shown here have passed through my hands and I have given them the same rigorous examination as those of the previous century. These chairs have a beauty of their own and their like is seen nowhere else in the world.

The Nineteenth Century

The Nineteenth Century

The Nineteenth Century

(Opposite). Stamped J Gabbitass (1822-39). Yew wood, elm seat. Gabbitass was possibly the first maker of Windsor chairs in Worksop. See *The English Regional Chair* by Bernard D. Cotton, pp. 168-169, for further study of the Gabbitass family of chair makers.

Three types of side chairs with triple splat formation in the back. Various woods – yew wood, fruitwood, ash – all seats are elm.

Five side chairs with single splats of different designs. All made of ash, beech and with elm seats. Attributed to Thames Valley and the Chilterns, circa 1840-60. All with an 'H' stretcher.

The Nineteenth Century

The Nineteenth Century

Paired armchairs, of lace Gothic design. One is of yew wood with a crinoline stretcher, the other of ash with an 'H' stretcher.

The Nineteenth Century

Pair of side chairs of lace Gothic design. Both made from ash with elm seats. Both have an 'H' stretcher.

(Opposite.)
A form previously unrecorded. Yew, ash, with an elm seat, circa 1830. It shows all the signs of probably having been made in the Mendlesham region.

Two armchairs with triple splat formation in back, one in yew wood with an elm seat and a crinoline stretcher, the other of ash with an elm seat and an 'H' stretcher. Both chairs attributed to Thames Valley and the Chilterns.

The Nineteenth Century

The Nineteenth Century

An elbow chair with a high back, surmounted by a very plain cresting rail and a central splat with a stylised wheel fret. The crook underarm supports, leg turnings and the fact that it is made of ash and beech with an elm seat probably indicate that it is from the High Wycombe area, circa 1840.

Similar to the chair opposite but with a higher back and lesser high quality turnings.

(Opposite.)
An all stick low-back elbow Windsor. Yew wood with an elm seat, circa 1830
Crinoline stretcher and crook underarm supports. The turnings are very fine. Also note the turnings on the crinoline retaining struts.

The Nineteenth Century

103

The Nineteenth Century

A series of double bow elbow chairs

High-back elbow chair. Yew wood. Crook underarm supports and a crinoline stretcher. The central splat has a fretted wheel design.

Similar but with a flower design fretted into the central splat. Yew wood. It has an 'H' stretcher and finer turnings.

Similar again, but yet another design in the central splat – a primitive fret of the Prince of Wales' feathers motif.

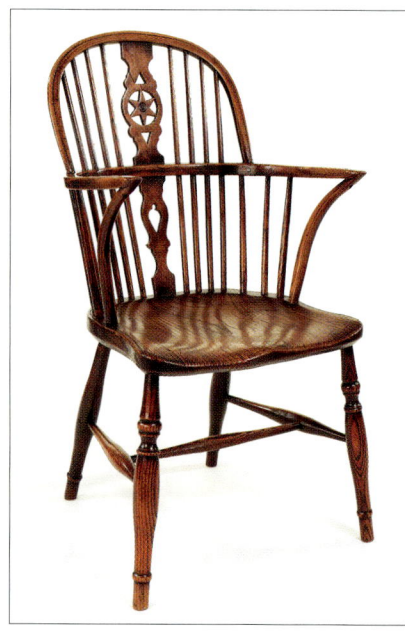

Both these chairs are similar again, but with a fretted six pointed star and a shield motif in the central splats.

The Nineteenth Century

(Above left.)
Similar again, with a blank domino or draught in the central splat.

(Above centre.)
Very large double bow elbow with Prince of Wales feathers fretted splat, crook underarm supports and heavily turned legs and stretcher.

(Above right.)
As the previous example. A very large double bow elbow chair, it has a highly decorated central splat plus the added attraction of the crinoline stretcher.

(Right.)
The most common of splat motifs, the wheel splat, in a double bow armchair. A Windsor high-back from the Thames Valley and Chilterns area made of various woods such as ash, fruitwoods, and beech, almost always with elm seat. There were also those called 'Best Chairs', which were made from yew wood. See opposite page, top left.

A rare style of chair generally known as a shawl-back. Yew wood, elm seat, circa 1800. Height 46in. (117cm), width 23in. (58cm)
The crest rail of a shawl-back chair bends about a third toward the front, thus creating a high curved back. The name might have come from a shawl or blanket being placed over the back to keep out draughts. It is certainly a good large chair and with a huge central splat makes a good fireside chair.

The Nineteenth Century

A double bow high-back elbow chair from the North-east part of England. Attributed to Nottinghamshire, possibly Worksop, circa 1840. Yew wood, elm seat. Height 44in. (112cm), width 23in. (58cm)
A very good example of the high quality achieved by chair makers. This fine chair is made of the best yew available (apart from the seat) and, when sold as new, would most certainly have been considered a 'Best Chair'.

The Nineteenth Century

The Nineteenth Century

(Opposite.)
A double bow high-back elbow chair. Attributed to Nottinghamshire, circa 1840. Yew wood, ash back legs, elm seat. Height 41in. (104cm), width 22in. (56cm) Similar to the previous chair but does not have its stature or finesse It is, however, a 'Best Chair' and is well made with a crinoline stretcher and very good turnings. This style of chair is often stamped with a maker's name and place of manufacture (or assembly).

A similar double bow yew wood high-back elbow chair.

A similar double bow, but this chair is made mainly from ash (elm seat) and the splat in the back and the turnings are of lesser quality.

The Nineteenth Century

Six yew wood triple splat armchairs matched to make an attractive set of dining chairs.

Eight ash side lace gothic chairs collected together for the same purpose.

The Nineteenth Century

A collection of five children's chairs, c.1850, among which the one below opposite is very unusual. This style of chair is often referred to as a correction chair. The five others are from the North-east region.

Child's chair.

High chair, yew wood.

The Nineteenth Century

(Above.)
High chair.

(Above left.)
Adolescent's chair, ash.

(Left.)
Correction chair, Chilterns region.

The Nineteenth Century

A collection of five different styles of yew wood low-backs, three from Nottinghamshire and two (lower left and opposite page) from Lincolnshire.

The Nineteenth Century

The Nineteenth Century

(Above.)
A pair of yew wood low-backs, stamped Amos Grantham.
This example of an early Amos chair is a refined and dynamic design, embodying the curved underarm support used in chairs made during the first third of the 19th century.

(Opposite.)
A original set of yew wood low-backs
This set of chairs is extremely rare as they are all stamped with the mark of the maker, Amos of Grantham (1814-42).

A matched set of superb yew wood high-back elbow chairs
The highly decorated splats and elaborately turned legs with almost hoof-like feet are similar to those by J. Gabbitass of Worksop (page 94).

The Nineteenth Century

Six yew wood low-back elbow matched to make a fine set of dining chairs.

119

The Nineteenth Century

All these 19th century chairs are in the collection of the Wycombe Museum
and are reproduced by courtesy of the Museum

(Above.) Child's Windsor high chair with fleur-de-lis splat.

(Above right.) Writing Windsor with arm rest.

(Right.) Scroll-back Windsor.

The Nineteenth Century

(Above.) Windsor commode chair and scroll-back high chair.

(Above right.) Scroll-back Windsor with carved back rest.

(Right.) Windsor armchair of simple form.

(Far right.) Lath-back Windsor with elaborate splat.

The Nineteenth Century

![settee]

A late 19th century settee which is over 7ft. (2.1m) long. The turnings in the back and legs are of the highest standard and it was probably specially made to stand in the entrance of a public building. It is mostly made of mahogany, although the seat is of one single piece of elm. It is truly a magnificent piece of Victorian utilitarian furniture.

(Right and opposite.) Atmospheric pictures of six yew wood low-back and two high-back elbow chairs, all of which are stamped Nicholson Rockley (the stamp of George Nicholson of Rockley, 1831-41). See *The English Regional Chair* by Bernard D. Cotton, pp. 183-186 for further study.

The Nineteenth Century

123

The Nineteenth Century

Side view.

(Opposite.)
An Arts and Crafts Movement chair, circa 1890. Oak. Height 35½in. (90cm). Seat diameter 16in. (41cm).

Detail showing carving on the back of the arm bow.

Detail of seat showing the carving around the seat.

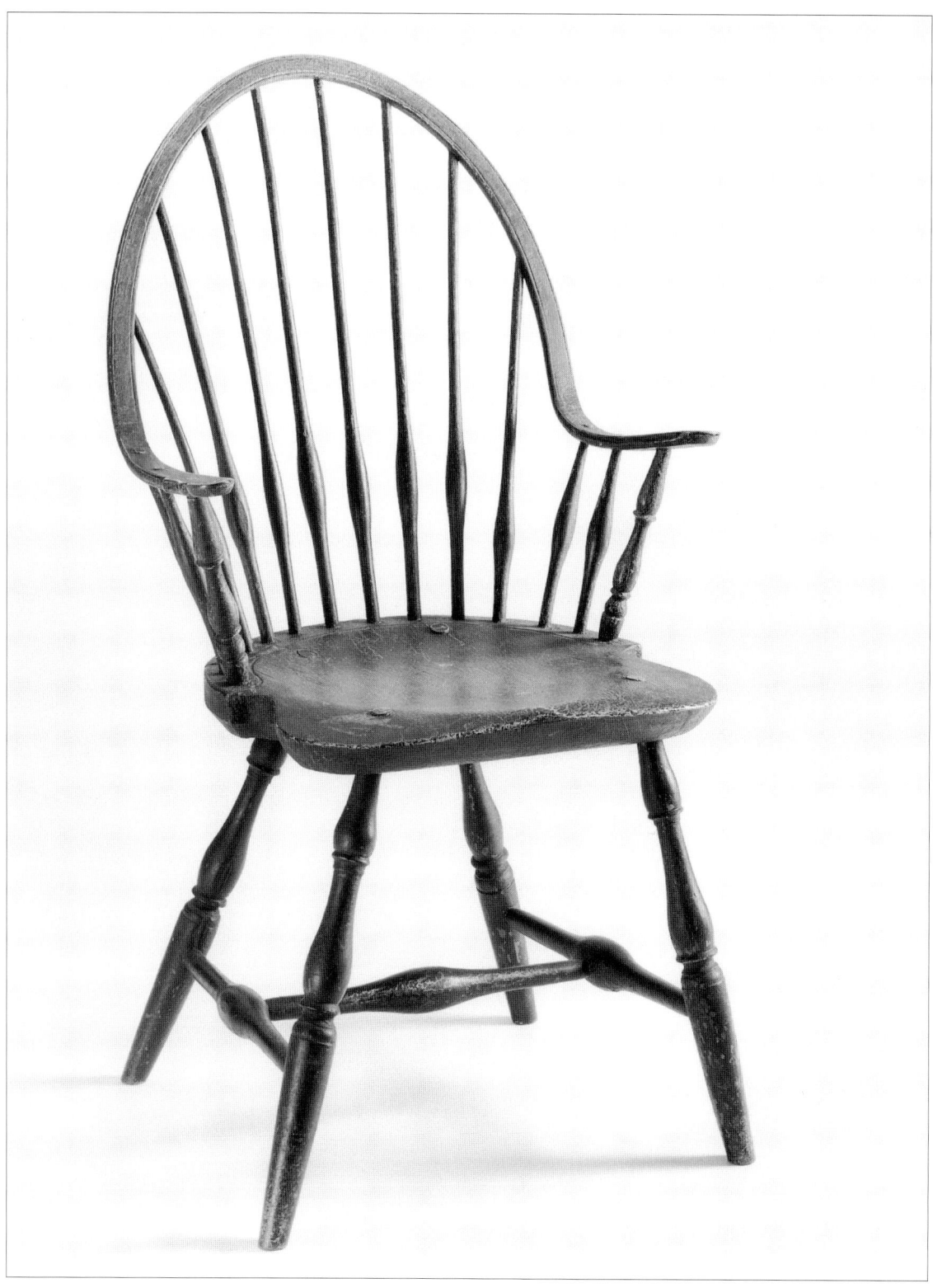

THE AMERICAN WINDSOR

In contrast to the English Windsor chair I have handled far fewer American Windsors and I have enlisted the help of a few specialised dealers on the East Coast of America where the American Windsor's unique style probably first appeared. I have in this case used as my main source of reference American Windsor Chairs *by Nancy Goyne Evans, who was formerly on the staff at the Henry Francis du Pont Winterthur Museum. I highly recommend it to those who wish to make a serious study of the American Windsor.*

When the Windsor chair first made its appearance in Britain, America consisted of thirteen colonies comprised mostly of rural settlements with a handful of cities and a larger number of towns spread along the Eastern Seaboard.

It was impractical to send goods overland and most goods travelled either by river or up and down the coast by sea. Most manufactured items, at least up to the War of Independence, were imported from England. The road systems posed such limitations that examples of Windsor chairs from England would have reached some of the fledgling states before their citizens saw examples from the state next to them.

The citizens of the then colonies would have first seen English Windsor chairs as they arrived as part of the furnishings of wealthy colonists, as mentioned in Nancy Goyne Evans' *American Windsor Chairs.* 'When Patrick Gordon arrived in Philadelphia in 1726 as Lieutenant Governor under Penn family sponsorship, he probably brought sufficient furnishings befitting his position. His 1736 estate inventory documents a substantial household, including "Five Windsor Chairs" valued at 11s.6d apiece.' At the same time English Windsors were being used as part of the furnishing of ships that called at the ports.

Over a period of a few years shipping and new immigrants between them must have supplied examples of most styles available in England.

It was most unlikely that the early chair makers could have examined books of designs for inspiration, as these probably did not circulate until the mid-eighteenth century, even in England.

The substantial increase in the population would have led to a steady demand, but a difference of design was quickly established. The American Windsor is very much a specialised chair with quite individual characteristics. It took aspects of the English design and added stylised variations from a different tradition. The angle of joining the legs into the seat plank was different and,

---

Opposite: A continuous-bow American Windsor armchair. Circa 1790-1800, Hickory, ash, white pine and maple. Height 37⅜in. Width 22in. Attributed to Rhode Island, USA

This style of Windsor chair is most elegant. A chair of this design was also made in England, where they appear to have been restricted to Yealmpton, Devonshire. They were painted in drab colours, one supposes for use in the garden. The American versions were popular in New York, Rhode Island and part of Connecticut. The continuous arm Windsor chair is as popular today in America and is still made in great quantities. It is a design of which Wallace Nutting wrote in 1917: *we could see no way of improvement.*

COURTESY WINTERTHUR MUSEUM

although the basic construction and build method were the same, there was a much more consistent utilitarian approach to making chairs. For instance, very rarely do you see a central splat as this was probably considered to be an unnecessary embellishment.

Timber was not a problem. America had a variety of native indigenous woods of great abundance and, as in England, the craftsmen favoured various woods for the separate parts of the chair.

The seats were in the main made from pine; being softwood it had the advantage of being easy to shape. Maple was the principal wood used for turnings, the bentwork is most frequently of oak, the spindles are often of hickory. Of course there were regional differences and the illustrations that follow show that different colonies favoured wood that was ready available to them. For example, chestnut was used in some Rhode Island and Connecticut seats, but not elsewhere. As the early chairs were mostly painted, as in England, other available regional woods could be used.

By the 1770s the American Windsor had become the most prolific item of furniture ever to be made in that country.

When in 1796 George Washington purchased from Philadelphia Windsor chair makers Robert and Gilbert Gaw twenty-seven bow-back Windsor side chairs at $1.78 each for use on the portico of his Mount Vernon home, he chose the American design. Such valuable patronage by a revered figure guaranteed popularity.

Another founding father, John Adams (1733-1826), second President of the United States of America, had as his favourite chair an American designed Windsor. Legend has it that Thomas Jefferson, the third President of the U.S.A., composed the first draft of the Declaration of Independence while sitting on an unusual swivel type of American Windsor chair from Philadelphia. The first and second Continental congresses sat in Windsors while they discussed the government of the new nation.

The same reasons that made the Windsor chair so appealing to the founders of America all those years ago make it just as popular today. Major American and English furniture companies still produce thousands of Windsor chairs a year and each year the demand for Windsors seems to increase. Wallace Nutting's reasoning, when writing in 1917, is still relevant: 'The Windsor has held its popularity steadily for two centuries in its original or debased forms. No other style of furniture has been so persistent and kept its quiet place while others styles came and went. It is the lightest of chairs, but its merit is its beauty. Though its lines are so simple, it is at its best very dignified, attractive and decorative. It is truly an aristocrat among chairs'.

A sack-back American Windsor armchair, with top extension. Circa 1770-1810. Ash, birch and basswood. Height 44½in. Width 23¼in. Depth 26½in. Attributed to New England, USA. Another example of an extension comb, this time rising above a bow, more common than the triple tall back, but still very rare.

COURTESY WINTERTHUR MUSEUM, GIFT OF CHARLES K. DAVIS

A triple tall back American Windsor armchair. Circa 1770-1810. Ash, birch, white pine and white oak. Height 45in. Width 25⅞in. Depth 16¼in. This chair illustrates how American chair makers produced highly innovative patterns for special orders or limited markets. I have only ever seen one English Windsor with an extension to the back row.   COURTESY WINTERTHUR MUSEUM

The American Windsor

Fan-back Windsor side chair. Massachusetts, circa 1780. Mixed woods, with old or original black paint with gilt decoration.   COURTESY OF DAVID A. SCHORSCH AMERICAN ANTIQUES, INC.

The American Windsor

Rare fan-back Windsor side chair with Queen Anne pad feet. New York City, circa 1785. Mixed woods, with an old refinished surface. One of only three known American Windsor chairs having Queen Anne pad feet.
COURTESY OF DAVID A. SCHORSCH AMERICAN ANTIQUES, INC.

The American Windsor

Fan-back Windsor armchair. Attributed to Charles Chase (1731-1813). Nantucket, Massachusetts, circa 1790. Mixed woods, with late 19th century black paint with yellow pinstriped decoration over green and white paint. Descended in the Coffin family of Nantucket until 1999.

Courtesy of David A. Schorsch American Antiques, Inc.

A rare and unusual black-painted bow-back Windsor side chair. Connecticut-Rhode Island border region, circa 1795-1805. Mixed woods, retains the original black paint.
The embryonic ears of this chair appear on only three other known examples.

COURTESY OF WAYNE PRATT, INC.

The American Windsor

Red-painted writing-arm fan-back Windsor. Connecticut, circa 1780-1790. Mixed woods, in pristine condition, retaining the original red-painted surface. COURTESY OF WAYNE PRATT, INC.

The American Windsor

One of a rare set of six white-painted bamboo-turned Windsor side chairs. Attributed to James C. Tuttle, Salem, Massachusetts, circa 1800–1810. Mixed woods, retains the original white lead paint with black detailing.
COURTESY OF WAYNE PRATT, INC.

(Opposite.)
An extremely rare painted Windsor child's high chair. Connecticut-Rhode Island border region, circa 1800–1810. Mixed woods, vestiges of original paint throughout.
COURTESY OF WAYNE PRATT, INC.

A rare white-painted bamboo-turned settee. Attributed to James C. Tuttle. Salem, Massachusetts, circa 1800–1810. Mixed woods. This may be the only extant settee associated with Tuttle's shop.   COURTESY OF WAYNE PRATT, INC.

The American Windsor

A green-painted Windsor writing-arm chair. Attributed to Ebenezer Tracy (1744-1803). Lisbon, Connecticut, circa 1790-1810. Mixed woods, retains an old green painted surface.

COURTESY OF WAYNE PRATT, INC.

(Opposite.) A rare set of seven painted bow-back Windsor side chairs. Rhode Island, circa 1780-1800. Mixed woods, retains old 19th century black paint over the original green-painted surface.

COURTESY OF WAYNE PRATT, INC.

The Modern Tradition

WINDSOR CHAIRS

ABOVE

5138A Double bow wheelback armchair with crinoline stretcher.
Width: 1' 11½" (0.60m). Depth 2' 2" (0.66m) Height: 3' 3" (0.99m).

5138 Wheelback small chair to match.
Width: 1' 7½" (0.49m). Depth: 1' 9" (0.53m) Height: 2' 10" (0.86m).

5143A Double bow wheelback armchair with crinoline stretcher and cabriole legs.
Width: 2' ½" (0.62m). Depth: 2' 2½" (0.67m). Height: 3' 3½" (1.00m).

5143 Wheelback small chair to match.
Width 1' 7½" (0.49m). Depth: 1' 8½" (0.52m). Height: 2' 9½" (0.85m).

LEFT

5181A Gothic bow Windsor armchair.
Width 2' 0" (0.61m). Depth: 1' 11½" (0.60m). Height 3' 3½" (1.00m).

5181 Small chair to match.
Width: 1' 6" (0.46m). Depth: 1' 7½" (0.49m). Height: 3' 1½" (0.95m).

Dimensions: *The dimensions are approximate.*

Polishing shades: *Items are supplied in reproduction or distressed antique finishes and polished to clients' own shades if desired.*

All items are made by us in High Wycombe.

The Thomas Glenister Company
Established 1839
Hughenden Road, High Wycombe, England.   Telephone: (0494) 21988

Ref. 94

THE MODERN TRADITION

The traditions of the nineteenth century have carried on into the twentieth and twenty-first centuries and we must not neglect the small selection of high quality chairs that this era has produced.

In 1939 the need for the chair industry to play its part in the war effort meant a massive upheaval and all productive effort was organised by the government. Labour could be 'directed' and materials commandeered. The resultant surge in production placed High Wycombe chairs in every officers' mess, service canteen (NAAFI) and government department in the land.

An early 20th century settee in the Windsor form, probably from one of the High Wycombe workshops.

(Opposite.)
Advertising from The Thomas Glenister Company, High Wycombe, 1950s.

The Modern Tradition

142

The Modern Tradition

(Left above.)
Old chair workshop in West Wycombe, now a conservation area.

(Left below.)
Glenister's factory before being pulled down to make way for a supermarket.

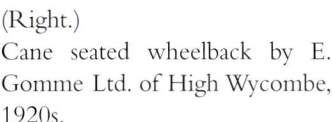

(Right.)
Cane seated wheelback by E. Gomme Ltd. of High Wycombe, 1920s.
COURTESY WYCOMBE MUSEUM

This period also saw the introduction of 'Utility' furniture; this was government-inspired furniture made to a basic design with whatever materials could be afforded. Furniture was rationed and available only to those issued with the necessary coupons. Utility furniture, including simple Windsor variants, was produced up to the 1950s when rationing was abolished. After this time a crop of fresh Windsor chair designs emerged, produced by Messrs Glenister's and E. Gomme Ltd., among others. By the '90s intense international competition, mainly from Eastern Europe, decimated the industry and the last specialist Windsor chair making factory, Glenister's, closed in the 1990s and was demolished to make way for a supermarket.

The Ercol Company, however, which makes a wide range of furniture, continues to make Windsor chairs in large numbers in the twenty-first century. Lucian Ercolani was born in San Angelo, Vado, Italy, the son of a woodcarver. The family came to Britain in 1898 and Lucian studied at the Shoreditch Technical Institute and became a freelance furniture designer and draughtsman.

The Modern Tradition

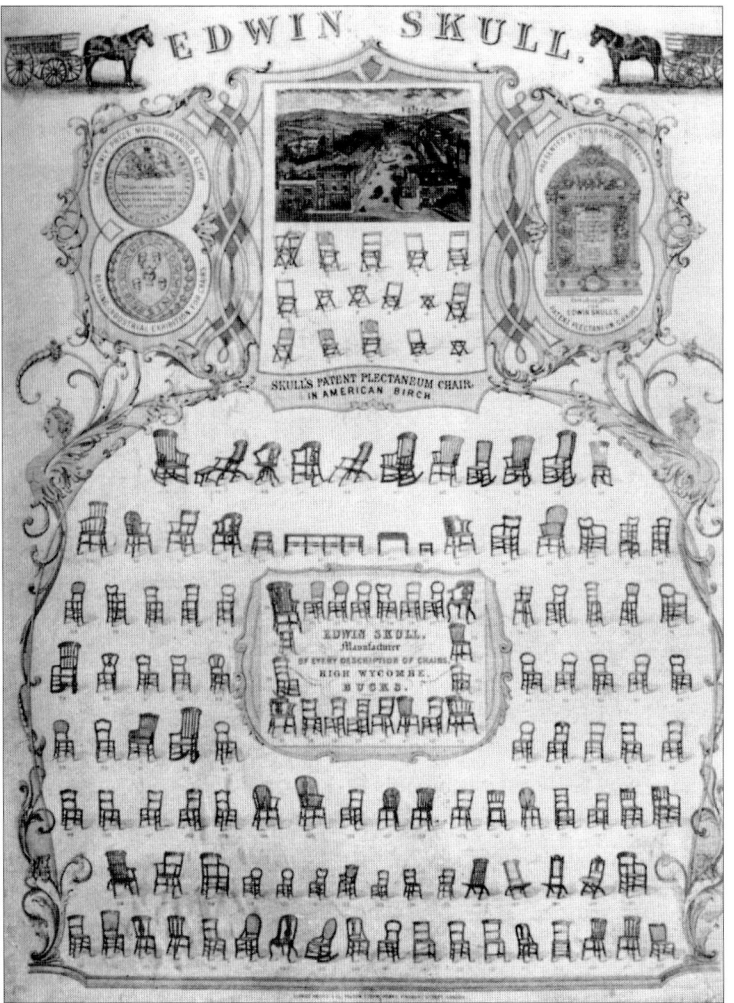

The display card used by Edwin Skull of High Wycombe, 1865-70. The variety of chairs is outstanding, with many variants of Windsor such as high and low bowbacks, wheelbacks, splatbacks and, in addition, smoker's bow, scroll, lath, spindle, Gothic scroll, lath-and-splat, rocking and steamer chair varieties. COURTESY JOHN ANDREWS

(Opposite.)
Ercol Windsor chair.

In 1910 he moved to High Wycombe to work for Frederick Parker and then Gomme's before setting up his own factory with twenty men in 1920. 'Furniture Industries Limited' made steady progress and gained a reputation for good quality work. In 1934 it absorbed one of the oldest local businesses, Walter Skull & Son, established in 1813 by Charles Skull who was followed by Edwin and various other family members. Skull was maintained as a separate unit making its own lines until the 1950s when the upholstery work and the manufacture of most of the chairs was shifted to the old Skull factory on Queen's Road.

What set Ercol apart from the other large Wycombe companies was the dominating presence of Lucian Ercolani who not only kept quality in the factory in line but also controlled the design process and masterminded every aspect of the company's life, at least until the mid-1960s. The main innovation was the decision to make an updated version of the Windsor chair, which possibly grew out of the chunky Windsors which were made as part of the Utility range. Together with the Furniture Research Laboratory at Princes Risborough, Ercol developed a method of drying and joining elm in a way to keep it flat, which opened the way to mass machine-production of the Windsor and a

modernisation in its design. This fitted in with Ercolani's belief that his furniture should be craftsmanlike and affordable, and led to an overwhelming emphasis on the virtue of solid wood. This was not always commercially advantageous. The 'Chairmaker's Chair', a modernised Windsor high-back armchair with sweeping arm-bow, is arguably one of the most elegant chairs ever made, but very few were ever sold – it remains a prestige piece rather than a profit-making one.

The greatest innovation in terms of production was the introduction of computer-controlled machinery from the late 1980s onwards. This makes manufacture easier, although it constrains somewhat the form of the product (the carved motifs on the splats of Windsors, for instance, have to be designed around the capabilities of the router), and also means that hand-carving is now virtually redundant, leaving framing and polishing as the only traditional skills that are still needed in mass-produced items.

In the early 1990s it became clear that, if expansion and reorganisation was to take place, Ercol would have to move from its existing factory which had grown piecemeal over the previous seventy years. The move from Wycombe to Princes Risborough took place in 2002.

The Modern Tradition

Jack Goodchild in his workshop making a Gothic fretted splat.   COURTESY WYCOMBE MUSEUM

Goodchild chair c.1950.   COURTESY WYCOMBE MUSEUM

Among the last individual chair makers of note was Jack Goodchild who worked from a workshop next to his house in Naphill, a few miles from High Wycombe. His father was an adzer of chair seats, but Jack Goodchild learned to make the whole chair himself, from felling the timber to the final polishing. There can be few people who knew more about the Windsor chair. He repaired and made chairs to order for over fifty years until his death in 1950. His chairs were certainly popular and H.J. Massingham is quoted as saying that he had to wait for over two years for delivery. There is no doubt that Jack Goodchild is and always will be the most renowned chair maker of his time.

(Opposite.)
Windsor chair made by Jack Goodchild for the writer, H.J. Massingham, in the early 1940s, and about which he wrote in his book *Men of Earth*.

The Modern Tradition

The Modern Tradition

(Opposite.)
Birch chair, mahogany, c.1900. The Birch Design and Cost Book entry for this chair is shown below.

(Below.)
The entry in the Birch Design and Cost Book showing the cost of producing the chair illustrated opposite. COURTESY WYCOMBE MUSEUM

Birch's pricing code.

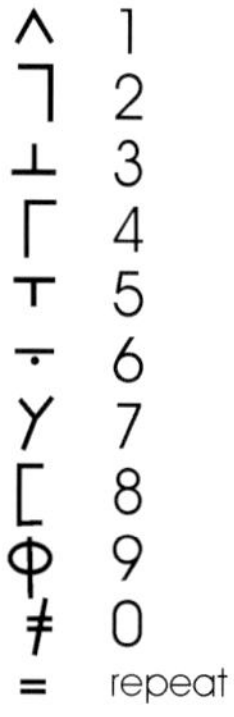

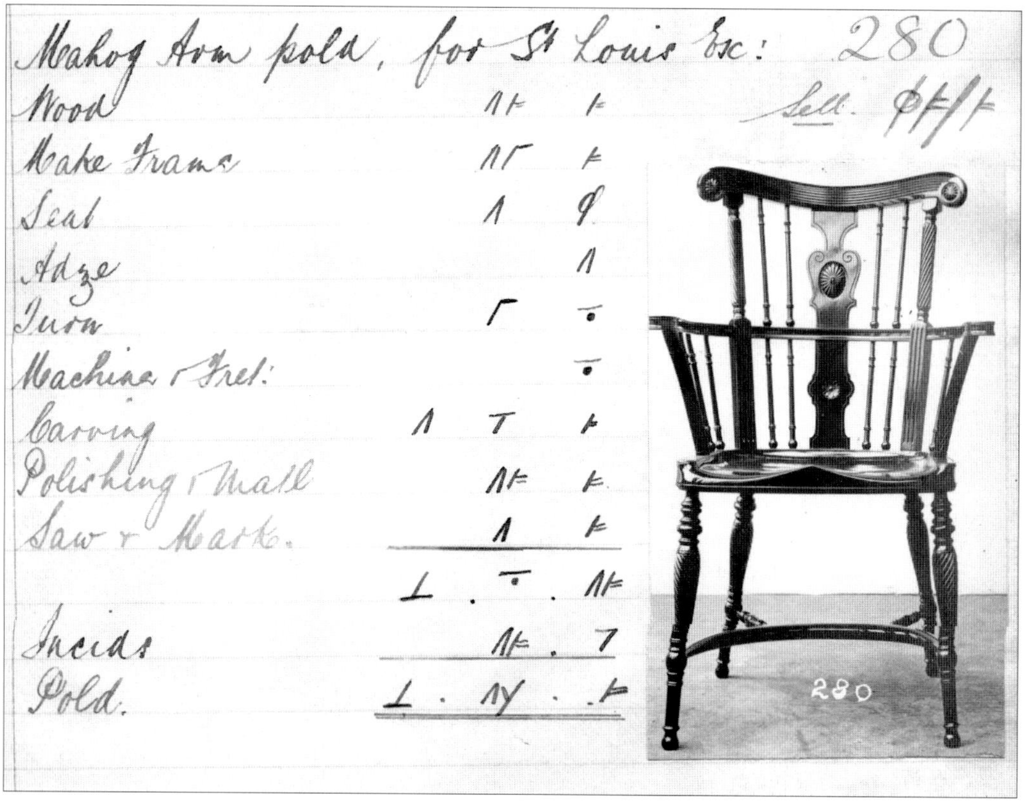

The firm of William Birch & Co. first appears in trade directories in 1853 in Newland, but family tradition states that Birch began chairmaking in the 1840s. In 1883 William's son, Walter Birch, started his own chairmaking business in Castle Street, after beginning some years before at the back of the Woolpack public house in Oxford Road. Walter had taken over his father's firm by 1895, when it appears as 'Birch & Company' with premises in Denmark Street.

The Modern Tradition

Birch's was one of a number of Wycombe firms that pioneered the move from standard cheap Windsor and rush or cane-seated furniture to a higher class of manufacture. It made a vast range of hybrid forms, including Arts & Crafts and Art Nouveau styles, particularly as a result of using designers such as E.G. Punnett and George Walton who had worked in the Mackintosh studio in Glasgow. Many lines were specifically produced for Liberty's and other leading London stores, and the firm maintained an office in Euston Road for many years. The Denmark Street factory was rebuilt as a three-storey, all-brick building in about 1898 to counter the risk of fire but itself burned down within a few months of being built!

After a strike in its London workshop in 1897, Birch's shifted the balance in its upholstery shop to the Wycombe site and recruited upholsterers and other craftsmen from all across the country. These in turn set up the town's first branch of the National Amalgamated Furniture Trades Association and Birch's became a modernising employer as well as manufacturer. The company opened a second Wycombe site in Leigh Street, where the business was concentrated between 1931 and 1935. By 1938 it employed 350 people. Birch's was taken over by Gomme's in 1954.

(Opposite.)
Close-up of the back of the Birch chair on page 149 showing the elaborately turned sticks, outer supports and carved splat.

(Left.)
Close-up of the arm of the Birch chair.

The Modern Tradition

There are still a small number of manufacturers making Windsor chairs in the Thames Valley. Prominent among these is Stewart Linford, working in the old Kitchener workshops in High Wycombe which originally housed Birch and Alpe (see pages 152 and 153).

Golden Jubilee chair by Stewart Linford. Yew wood.

Stewart Linford, who started on his own in 1976 and now has a large thriving business, uses traditional methods of making furniture. As well as chairs of all types he still favours the traditional Windsor in its eighteenth century form and made with eighteenth century methods. He works mostly in British hardwoods and yew, but some North American hardwoods, notably maple, are also used. Despite Dutch elm disease, Linford has a good stock of this beautiful timber and is still able to make Windsor chairs with seats made out of solid blocks of two-inch thick English elm. He is a founder member of the Woodland Heritage, an organisation set up to improve the way in which trees, particularly broad-leaf, are grown, maintained and harvested in the U.K., and to expand the area of woodland.

All Stewart Linford furniture is stamped with his signature and carries his lifetime guarantee. He is a Liveryman of the Worshipful Company of Furniture Makers and a Freeman of the City of London.

Stewart Linford 'chairing up'.

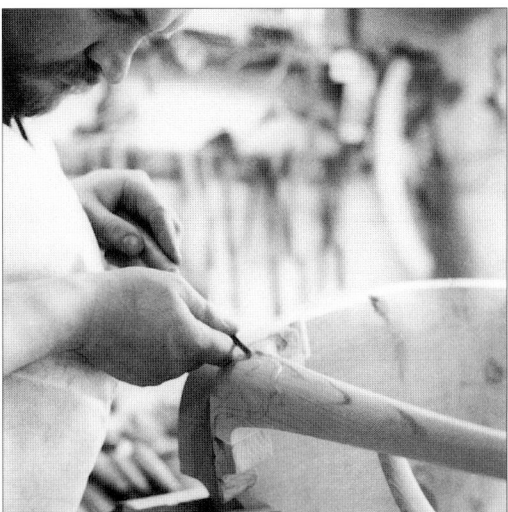

Stewart Linford carving a cabriole leg.

The Modern Tradition

The Millennium chair by The Real Wood Furniture Company. Fruitwood.

Glossary

Adapted from *The Windsor Chair* by Thomas Crispin

Adze – Curved and saucered form of axe, used to create the saddle-shaped wooden seat of the Windsor chair.

Arm-bow – A curved section of wood made from supple wood, steamed, then bent around a former. Can also be cut from the solid and shaped in two or three sections, as in the Goldsmith chair (see page 20).

Arm-bow support – The support which stretched from the seat to the arm-bow. It could be turned, cut from the solid, or shaped as a half crinoline stretcher and raised vertically.

Back-stays – Stays at the back of the Windsor chair to the top cresting rail of the comb-back or the bow of the bow-back chair.

Bob-tail – The small extension to the seat of the Windsor chair in which the bracing sticks, back-stand and back-stays are housed.

Bodger – A local name in Buckinghamshire for a chair leg turner, who also makes the 'stretchers' and the 'sticks' (*see also* pole lathe).

Bodleian – Name given to a comb-back, stick Windsor chair, originally supplied to the Bodleian Library, Oxford (see pages 14, 28 and 29).

Bow-back chair – A Windsor chair in which the back-sticks and splat are housed and contained within a curved bow.

Comb-back chair – A Windsor chair in which the back-sticks are housed into the top cresting rail, giving the illusion of a large comb.

Crest rail – The top rail of a Windsor comb-back chair. Also the technical term used for the top rail of any chair.

Crinoline stretcher – A curved stretcher of semi-circular form, extending between the two front legs. It is supported at its back by two short turned stretchers, which are jointed into the back legs. Also referred to as a cow-horn stretcher and a spur stretcher.

Fan-back – A type of comb-back Windsor chair where the comb above the seat is fanned out towards the top cresting rail.

Gothic Windsor chair – A type of bow-back Windsor chair, the back designed in a similar shape to the 'Gothic' windows of Walpole's 'Strawberry Hill' house. The backs are mostly stickless, support being ensured by the central splat, and a system of minor ones, all of them pierced and shaped in the 'Gothic' style of c.1770. The back-bows of some, being exaggerated in the 'Gothic' taste, are assembled of two bows joined at an acute angle at the top. A simple one-piece bow-back is found upon other examples, with a pierced 'Gothic' splat (*see also* interlaced-bow chairs).

Goldsmith chair – A type of comb-back Windsor armchair with stick-back, round saddled seat and bob-tail. The sticks are very slightly fanned out and the legs are turned. Originally owned by Oliver Goldsmith (1728-1774), the writer, hence the name. See page 20.

'H'–stretcher – The conventional Windsor chair stretcher The two outside stretchers unite the legs by a central stretcher, the resultant frame forming the letter 'H'.

'Hoof' foot – A 'goat's hoof' attached to the end of a cabriole leg.

Lace Gothic – a type of bow-back Windsor with the back designed to a 'Gothic' shape. Made in the late 18th and early 19th centuries. The style of the back owes its influence to the glazing bars of Walpole's 'Strawberry Hill' house at Twickenham (*see* pages 98, 99 and 111).

Mendlesham chair – An East Anglian Windsor chair thought to originate from the Mendlesham area. In the design the traditional bow-back has been supplanted with a Sheraton style square-back but with the turned legs, pierced splat, stick-back and arms (where applicable) which are all traditional Windsor chair parts. The craftsmanship of the construction is mostly superb; the best woods, yew and fruitwood, were used, with restrained boxwood inlay. Some of these chairs have been attributed to a Richard Day, who worked as a chairmaker at Mendlesham in Suffolk, c.1830. *See* pages 90-91.

Glossary

Painting – The Windsor chair, when originally made for use in the garden, was painted either black or dark green. In the 18th century these paints were made from the whey of milk, which formed a lactic acid to which a primary colour would be added as a pigment.

Pole lathe – A primitive but surprisingly efficient lathe, operated by the turner with simple tools to produce turned parts of the Windsor chair. The pole consisted of a young larch or ash, grown to the right height and thickness, peeled of its bark, allowed to season and shaved on the underside to make it more pliable. A length of cord would be dropped from the pole to the lathe, fixed around the work to be turned and fastened to the treadle of the lathe. As the treadle was pressed down, the cord moved down also, causing the article to be turned to revolve and the pole to bend like a bow as the cord tightened. When the treadle was released, the pole sprang back into its original position, again rotating the article. As the motion was speeded up, the turner was able to shave away the surplus wood with a chisel and so shape the required article. The pole lathe was in operation in medieval times, turners arriving with the Norman Conquest. (*See also* bodger.)

Ribbon splat – A thin, straight-edged piece of timber, which runs from the crest rail through the arm-bow and is mortised into the seat. It often forms the outer post of the comb-back style Windsor chair.

Staining – Loudon (1784-1843) quotes on Windsor chairs: 'These chairs are sometimes painted, but are more frequently stained with dilute sulphuric acid and logwood, or by repeatedly washing them over with alum water, which has some tartar in it. They should afterwards be washed over several times with an extract of brazil wood. The colour given will be a sort of red, not unlike that of mahogany and, by afterwards oiling the chair and rubbing it well and for a long time with woollen cloths, the veins and shading of the elm will be rendered conspicuous. Quicklime, slaked in urine and laid on the wood while hot, will also stain it a red colour and this is said to be the general practise with the Windsor chair manufacturers in the neighbourhood of London'. J.C. Loudon *Encyclopaedia of Cottage Farm, and Villa Architecture and Furniture,* 1833. Brazil wood is mentioned by Evelyn in *Sylvia,* stating that plum tree 'approaches nearest beauty to brazil'. Sheraton states 'wood is imported for the dyers who use it much'. Logwood was in use as a dye wood since the 17th century and was recommended by Stalker and Parker in their *Treatise* (1688).

Stick-back Windsor – The terminology used to describe either a comb-back or bow-back Windsor chair with no decoration in the back, except vertical sticks.

Stretcher – The turned member which is used as a strengthener and stabiliser in the underframe of a chair between the legs. It can be of two, three or four members and employed in a parallel, quadrilateral or diagonal position, or forming the letter 'H' (*see* 'H'-stretcher, crinoline stretcher).

Tablet form Windsor – A Windsor chair with a plain, flat, top rail, often associated with scroll Windsor chairs, c.1840-60.

Thames Valley – A region extending from the Thames estuary to the Solent, taking in the counties of Buckinghamshire, Berkshire, London and part of Surrey. It encompasses the following proven districts where named Windsor chairmakers operated: London, Slough, Newington, Uxbridge, High Wycombe and West Wycombe.

Turner – *see* bodger, pole lathe.

Woods

Ash – A whitish-grey fairly hard wood used in Windsor chairmaking for arm-bow supports, bows, cresting rails, legs, sticks, stretchers and splats.

Beech – A light-brown surface wood with flecked grain used in Windsor chairmaking for arm-bow supports, legs, sticks and stretchers.

Cherry – A pale wood which matures to deep red, used in Windsor chairmaking for arm-bow supports, legs, splats, sticks and stretchers.

Elm – Brown with distinctive, blackish figuring in which the grain seems to run everywhere, nearly always used in Windsor chair seats.

Walnut – Pale brown, the principal wood of the 17th and early 18th century used for arm-bows, arm-bow supports and top bows (mainly 18th century chairs).

Yew – Reddish-brown, very hard wood with some burr effects used in Windsor chairmaking for arm-bow supports, bows, legs, splats, sticks and stretchers.

Select Bibliography

Agius, Pauline, *101 Chairs,* Antique Collectors' Club, 1968

Baylis, Chris, 'Thames Valley Windsor Chairs', Thames Valley Antique Dealers' Association Exhibition paper, March 1998

Cotton, B.D., *The English Regional Chair,* Antique Collectors' Club, 1990

Crispin, Thomas, 'English Windsor Chairs. A Study of Known Makers and Regional Centres', *Furniture History Society* (Vol. 14), 1978

Crispin, Thomas, *The Windsor Chair* (CINOA prizewinner 1991), Alan Sutton, 1992

Edwards, Ralph, *History of the English Chair,* 1951

Edwards, R./Macquoid, *Dictionary of English Furniture (Shorter),* Country Life

Ercol Paper, Wycombe Museum

Ercolani, Lucian, *A Furniture Maker,* Ernest Benn Ltd., 1975

Evans, Nancy Goyne, 'A History Background of English Windsor Furniture', *Furniture History Society* (Vol. 15)

Evans, Nancy Goyne, *American Windsor Chairs,* Hudsons Hills Press, New York, 1996

Evans, Nancy Goyne, 'A Guide to Eighteenth Century Windsor Chairs', *The Catalogue of Antique and Fine Art,* Spring 2002

Gilbert, Christopher, *Town & Country Furniture to Common Furniture,* Temple Newsam, 1972/82

Gilbert, Christopher, *English Vernacular Furniture 1750-1900,* published for the Paul Mellon Centre for Studies in British Art by Yale University Press, New Haven and London, 1991

Gilbert, Christopher, *Selected Writings on Vernacular Furniture 1966-98,* Regional Furniture Society, 2001

Gloag, John, *The Englishman's Chair,* 1964

Hayden, Arthur, *Chats on Cottage & Farmhouse Furniture,* T. Fisher Unwin Ltd., 1950

Massingham, H.J., *Men of Earth. The Chair Maker,* Chapman & Hall Ltd., 1943

Massingham, H.J., *Where Man Belongs.. Goodchild of Naphill,* Collins, 1946

Nutting, Wallace, *A Windsor Handbook,* 1917, Old American Co., Boston, Massachusetts, reprinted by Charles E. Tuttle Co., Rutland, Vermont

Ormsbee, Thomas H., *The Windsor Chair,* Deerfield Books Inc., 1962

Parker Knoll, *Collection, 1952-54,* Parker Knoll, 1951

Riley, Noël, 'The Mysterious Mendlesham Chair', *Country Life,* 24 June 1976

Rowe, F. Gordon, *English Cottage Furniture,* Phoenix House, 1952

Rowe, F. Gordon, *The Windsor,* Phoenix House, 1953

Sparks Ivan G., *The Windsor Chair,* Spur Books, 1975

Sparks Ivan G., *English Windsor Chairs,* Shire Books, 1981

INDEX

Page numbers in bold type refer to captions and illustrations

Adams, John, 128
Allsop, J., 88
Alpe, 151
America, 126-139
Amos of Grantham, **116-117**
Arts and Crafts Movement, **124-125**, 150
Art Nouveau, 150

Beaconsfield, 11
Birch & Co., William, 148-151 **148-151**
Birch, Walter, 148
Bodleian Library, **29**, 92, **92-93**
   Curator's Room, **12-13**, 13, 21
Bradshaigh, Sir Roger and Lady, **10-11**
Brown, John, 17
Buckinghamshire, 11

carving, **64-66**, 71
'Chairmaker's Chair', 145
Chase, Charles, **133**
Chilterns, **53**, **96-97**, **100**, **105**, **113**
'Chippendale' style, **22**, **54-56**, **58**, **60**, **68**, **74-75**, **80-81**
Coffin family, **133**
Connecticut, **126-127**, 128, **134**, **135**, **136-137**, **139**
Cook, Captain, **18-19**

D'Albiac family, **46-47**
Day family, of Mendlesham, 90-91
Devonshire, **126-127**
Durham, 23

Earle, Augustus, **20-21**
Eilean Donan Castle, **86**, 88, **88**
Ercol Company, 143-145, **145**
Ercolani, Lucian, 143-145

Furniture Industries Limited, 144
Furniture Research Laboratory, 144

Gabbitass, Elizabeth, 87
Gabbitass, John, 87, **87**, **94-95**, **118**
Gateshead, 23
Gaw, Robert and Gilbert, 128
George III, King, 11
Glasgow, 145
Glenister Company, Thomas, 92, **92, 140-142**, 143
Godfrey, J., 88
Golden Jubilee chair, **152**
Goldsmith, Oliver, 20, **20**
Gomme Ltd, E., 143-144, **143**, 150
Goodchild, Jack, 146, **146-147**
Gordon, Patrick, 127
Gothic style, **22**, 23, **80-85**, **98-99**, **111**
Grantham, 87, 88, **88**, **116-117**

Hall Barn, 11
Harold of Seall, 91
Hawes, Sir Benjamin, 20
Hawes, William, MD, 20
Hawks, Captain R., 23
Haytley, Edward, **10-11**
Hazell, Stephen, 92, **92-93**
High Wycombe, 15, 87, 90, **91**, **102**, **140-141**, 141ff.

Industrial Revolution, 15

Jackson's Oxford Journal, **29**
Jacob, Edmund, 91
Jefferson, Thomas, 128

Kitchener workshops, 151

Leggat, 91
Liberty's, 150
Lincolnshire, 87, 89, **114-115**
Linford, Stewart, 151-153, **152-153**
Lisbon, Connecticut, **139**
Longridge, Thomas, 23

Mackintosh, Charles Rennie, 150
Massachusetts, **131, 133, 135-136**
Massingham, H.J., 146, **147**
Mendlesham, 89, 90-91, **90-91, 100-101**
Millennium chair, **154**
Mompesson House, Salisbury, **23, 24**
Mount Vernon, 128

Nantucket, **133**
Naphill, 146
National Amalgamated Furniture Trades
  Association, 150
New England, **128-129**
New York, **126-127, 132**
Nicholson, George, **122-123**
Nottinghamshire, 87, 89, **107-109, 114**
North of England, 88, **107, 112-113**
Nutting, Wallace, **126-127**, 128

Officer's chair, 89, **89**

Parker, Frederick, 144
Perceval Compton, arms of, **3, 47**
Percival, Lord, 11
Philadelphia, 128
Pitt, John, 18, **18-19**
Princes Risborough, 144-145
Punnett, E.G., 150

Real Wood Furniture Company, The, **154**
Rhode Island, **126-127**, 128, **134, 136-139**
Rockley, 87, **122-123**
Royal Humane Society, 20
Royal Navy, **20-21**, 21, 89

St Paul's Churchyard, London, 17
Salem, **136**

Scott of Diss, 91
Sheraton, Thjomas, 90, 91
Shoreditch Technical Institute, 143
Skull & Son, Walter, 144
Skull, Edwin, 144, **144**
Sleaford, 87
Slough, **18**
Stowe, **16-17,** 17
Strawberry Hill, 23
Suffolk, 89, **90-91**

Thames Valley, 11, *passim*
Tracy, Ebenezer, **139**
Tuttle, James C., **136, 137**
Twickenham, 23

Versailles, 11
Vulcan, 23

Walpole, Horace, 23
Walton, George, 150
Washington, George, 128
Webb and Bunce, **91**
Webb, William, **78**
West Country, **48, 69,** 89
West Wycombe, **142-143**
  Park, 13-14, **13-15**
Wilson, George, 88, **88**
Windsor, 11, **18**
  Great Park, 11
Woodland Heritage, 153
Worksop, 87-88, **94-95, 107, 118**

'X' frame, **78-79**

Yealmpton, **126-127**